Dialogues
with
Dogs

Dialogues
with
Dogs

Why Dogs Behave the Way They Do

Bruce Fogle DVM MRCVS

Little Books by Big Names™

First published in the United Kingdom in 2004 by Little Books Ltd,
48 Catherine Place, London SW1E 6HL

10 9 8 7 6 5 4 3 2 1

A CIP catalogue record for this book is available from the British Library.

ISBN: 1 904435 30 0

Many thanks to: Jamie Ambrose for editorial production and management,
Mousemat Design Limited for text design,
John Noble for indexing,
Imago for printing consultancy.
Printed and bound in Hong Kong.

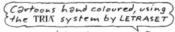

Cartoons hand coloured, using
the TRIA system by LETRASET

www. letraset.com

CONTENTS

INTRODUCTION

Your dog has one achievable aim in life. It wants to be in control: of itself and of you. All the nature and nurture, the evolution and learning, that goes into the make-up of your dog's mind is there to help it live a safe, secure, satisfying life. Dogs behave the way they do because they've inherited the malleable, plastic and inventive brain that evolved within the sociable and carnivorous canine family.

Dogs thrive on social interaction with other members of their own family. They can behave altruistically with that family, but they are also capable of savage ferocity. Most dogs excel in an environment where there is social order, but some want to upset that order – to challenge it if they feel they can gain greater control. Dogs learn from experience and are capable of learning throughout their lives, although as with so many other species (including ours), learning is easiest and most successful when they are young. Almost uniquely among carnivores, the dog evolved a range of behaviours that allowed it to adapt, survive and thrive within the human environment.

Over 2,700 years ago, in what is now modern Iran, the Persian Zoroastrians devoted one of the seven sacred books of their religion to dogs. In this ancient text the dog is described as having the character of a priest, a warrior, a livestock owner, a strolling singer, a thief, a wild beast, a courtesan and a child. If you're a dog owner, think about those descriptions and see how many apply to your dog or dogs you've known. Do you talk in confidence to your dog? Do you feel it protects you? Does your dog make you laugh or smile? Can it turn vicious? If it's a female, can she act like a tart, or if he's a male, does he behave like a testosterone-charged hunk? Does your dog depend on you?

The ancient Persians understood as well as we do today that dogs behave in radically different ways. That's not new. What is new is that today we have a better understanding of why dogs are capable of such a wide range of behaviours. That is what I'll discuss in the following pages, together with how to use that understanding to train dogs to become fully integrated members of our own human families.

'Are we going to stay independent, or hang out
with humans? To me, it's a no-brainer.'

chapter one
WHY DOGS CHOSE US

You may have read that 'Man domesticated the dog', but this statement is not true. We didn't intentionally create the dog; like the cat, the dog domesticated itself. Dogs probably descend from a single extended family of Asian wolves that discovered the benefits of living in close proximity to, and eventually within, human settlements. Over 12,000 years ago, wolf families successfully moved into the new ecological niche created by sites of permanent human settlement. (Some experts, using canine genetic markers, think this happened over a hundred thousand years ago – that wolves started to become domesticated when they became camp followers of nomadic human families.)

By 'successful' I mean that these wolves thrived, bred and perpetuated their genes. Their new 'man-made' environment had fewer hazards for wolves because people had already eliminated dangers such as other large predators. The land offered good scavenging and hunting, too, including the waste from the human community and the rodents attracted by that waste.

Survival of the fittest in these conditions favoured smaller wolves with less fear of people, wolves willing to sneak or creep near the settlements to eat waste or to trail human hunters and scavenge from their kills. With time – and it takes a surprisingly short time – several physical changes occurred in wolves. Without active human intervention in their breeding, the wolf became smaller, its teeth became more crowded and its brain shrank.

A smaller brain doesn't mean that a dog is less intelligent than a wolf. A dog's brain is about thirty percent smaller than the brain of a wolf of similar size, but this loss of size is restricted almost completely to the sensory parts of the brain. The thinking part – the cortex – didn't shrink with domestication. In that sense, the dog is no different from all other domesticated animals; when there is less need to map territory, hunt and forage, there's also less need to rely upon sight, scent and hearing.

Canine traits associated with domestication, such as smaller canine teeth, less aggression, a more varied diet, smaller brains and shorter intestines, are simply by-products of the distinctly new environmental pressures created by living near over-exploited sites of human habitation. The wolf-dogs best equipped to survive and breed in this man-made environment evolved, eventually with selective-breeding help from us, into the variety of morphologically and behaviourally distinct groups or breeds of dogs that exist today. Through our ancestors' eventual intervention to control wolf/dog breeding, we simply 'accelerated' natural evolution of the wolf to the dog.

This process of 'self-domestication' was possible because the *Canidae*, or canine, family, and that family includes the wolf, coyote and fox, had and still has a very plastic and inventive mind. Canines are capable of altering their lifestyles to take advantage of changes in the environment that people created.

In Britain, the fox did this in the latter part of the twentieth century by moving into towns and cities to scavenge from back gardens and throw-away convenience foods such as fried chicken and hamburgers. Russian studies in the 1980s showed that in only seven generations of selective breeding, foxes can become as tame as dogs, sitting on laps, coming when called, even barking like dogs.

In the United States and Canada, the coyote is doing the same today, spreading out of its traditional habitat in the Pacific west to survive and thrive in the east right to the edge of the Atlantic Ocean. (And, going technical for a moment, in case you've read that some dogs are descended from the coyote, genetic evidence all but discounts this possibility. While dogs and wolves share all but 0.2 percent of their mitochondrial DNA, there is a four percent difference in mitochondrial DNA – that is, the type of DNA which is passed through the female line – between coyotes and dogs.)

Where dogs come from

I think that there is only one known site where domestication of the wolf occurred, and this was somewhere in Asia. One reason I believe this is that nowhere are skeletons to be found of intermediate stages between the wolf and the dog. If domestication occurred spontaneously in a number of different locations, anthropological evidence should exist of these intermediate wolf/dog skeletons in Asia, North America, Africa and Europe. To date, no such evidence exists.

From Asia, via trade, migration and conquest, descendants of Asiatic wolves accompanied people as they migrated north, south, east and west. Domesticated Asian dogs arrived in Europe. They moved towards the north, where some mated with larger northern wolves, creating the root stock for indigenous Nordic breeds. Nordic dogs drifted back into the heartland of Europe, progenitors of the spitzes. Other dingo-like dogs accompanied Asian migrants across the Bering land bridge to the Americas, where some, such as the so-called

Carolina Dog, continued to breed true to their Asian origins while others crossbred with American wolves, creating the basis for breeds such as the Malamute and Eskimo dog. When Europeans arrived thousands of years later, other crossings occurred between these 'indigenous' dogs and the newer arrivals.

The history of the development of dog breeds is a history of the ebb and flow of isolated dog populations into new environments, where initially they may have mated with wolves, but latterly, they mated with resident dog populations. Our active intervention enhanced or diminished physical and psychological aspects of these populations. In doing so, we created the many breeds we have today.

Language clues to the dog's origins

Another reason I believe that all dogs came from one region has to do with linguistic clues about the dog's origins. Throughout the world, the words we use to specify 'dog' have a common phonetic root in ancient languages. In ancient Chinese, the word for dog is *k'iuon*. In ancient Japanese, it is *ken*. In Indo-European, which originated in the Indian subcontinent and is thought to be the ancestral language of most of Europe, the Middle East and India, the word for dog is *k'uon*. Thus, in ancient Greek it is *kyon*, while Latin *canis* has become Portuguese *cão*, Italian *cane*, Romanian *caine*, old Spanish *can* and French *chien*. Tribes in Siberia use the word *canac*, while in parts of east Africa the dog is called *kunano*.

In some languages, Indo-European 'k' evolved, or 'sound-shifted', into 'h'. So *Kuon* becomes *huon*, leading to the Dutch *hond*, German, Norwegian, Swedish and Danish *Hund* and English 'hound'. In other languages the 'k' became 'sh'. *Kuon* thus becomes *shuon*, evolving to the Sanskrit *shvan* and Armenian *shun*.

Although some languages have completely different words for 'dog' – for example, the Tamil *nay*, Finnish *koira* and Polish *psov* – the linguistic study of ancient root words suggests a common origin of domestication somewhere in Asia, with subsequent radiation in all directions.

'Toby! Off the sofa!'

People accentuated natural selection

The natural historian Stephen Jay Gould once wrote a fascinatingly perceptive scientific article called 'Walt Disney meets Konrad Lorenz', in which he suggested that Disney intuitively knew what Lorenz scientifically observed: that certain shapes triggered a parental response from us – for example, a round head with large round eyes. (This is why Disney intuitively changed the shape of Mickey Mouse's head from its original mouse-like shape to the rounded shape we're familiar with today.)

What's your reaction when you see a fox cub, a fawn, a calf, a piglet, a kitten or a dog pup? Well, orphaned or captured wolf pups were just as attractive to people 15,000 years ago as they are today. Women in particular were willing to play with abandoned wolf pups, even breast-feed them. These animals grew into ready meals for the community, but some escaped that fate and people discovered that adult wolves raised from puppyhood within a human environment were useful. If raised with humans, they did not as readily attack other people. They could also act as sentries. And in times of hunger, they still offered ready meat.

The first dogs to be born in human settlements bred on their own. The ones that were not eaten or used by adolescent boys for target practice became sentries, warning of danger. Unwittingly, people selected individual dogs for enhanced 'voice'. Barking was a bonus in sentry dogs.

Some of these settlement-bred and -raised wolf-dogs probably chose to accompany men (their adopted pack leaders) when they left the settlement to hunt. Men eventually observed that some dogs were faster or better at picking up an animal's scent trail than others. This added value saved them from the stew pot, and they lived long enough to mate and produce progeny that inherited their superior hunting ability.

No doubt there were thinking hunters thousands of years ago who, rather than letting their hunting companions breed with any of the other settle-ment-dog survivors, let them mate only with other excellent hunters. That was the true beginning of the dog's domestication by people. Natural-selection pressures created the dog out of the wolf, but it was when people realized that by breeding one dog with beneficial attributes with another having the same attributes that the dog's future became intertwined with that of people.

Why dogs look the way they do

Early breeding emphasized any practical uses for the dog, such as a willingness to join men in the hunt, acting as sight-hounds or scent-followers. Later, dogs were selectively bred for keenness to guard herds of sheep, goats and aurochs, the ancestors of modern cattle. In all of these circumstances, dogs were practical; they were useful to humans and were still a good source of meat when game became scarce. Survival of the fittest always favours those best-adapted to their environment.

Bantam and dwarf dogs

The dog's new ecological niche – living with people – now favoured the survival of curiosities, because people were and still are an intensely inquisitive species. We're intrigued by the weird, the grotesque, the outlandish or simply the cutesy.

Bantamization, or the production of perfectly formed, small versions of the parents, occurs infrequently, but it occurs naturally in virtually all species of plants and animals. Because of the original natural-selection pressures on wolves favouring the survival of smaller individuals, a genetic predisposition to smallness was probably already enhanced in wolf-dogs.

In most ecological situations, bantams don't survive. Bantam dogs, or 'miniatures', survived because they got extra help from people in the form of feeding, warmth and protection. When people gave extra help, they became more attached to these dogs; they were making more of an emotional investment in them. In return, the dogs were attached to the people because of the increased handling they received when very young. These dogs survived the dinner pot not just because they offered less meat, but also because they had become people's companions. From an evolutionary perspective, miniaturization in dogs was an extremely successful genetic shift.

A few words about dogs as food. We're repelled by statistics on dog-eating in China and the Philippines, but the practice is as old as our mutual relationship. In Mexico, for example, 5,000-year-old dog remains have been discovered. Some ancient Mexican tribes esteemed dogs as companions, guards and hunters. The Aztecs cremated dogs to be sent with the dead to act as guides on their continuing journeys. Others, however, associated dogs with promiscuity and filth, and while in some tribes, dog-eating was taboo, in others, dogs were virtually farmed for their meat. Examination of Olmec tribe refuse sites at San Lorenzo, Mexico, showed that seventy percent of mammal refuse consisted of dog bones. Carbon-isotope analysis of these bones showed that the dogs had eaten mostly maize, which suggests that either they were fed maize or they scavenged a whole lot of it. (When my son's black Lab, Inca, had pups, my daughter Tamara, who took a pup, mulled over naming the pup Maya. If she'd known that the Maya ate dogs on ceremonial days, she may or may not have had second thoughts. The pup got named Lola.)

A malfunction of the pituitary gland occasionally occurs in all mammals, with the result that a dwarf individual is produced. A dwarf pup is completely normal except that its leg bones are dramatically shortened and it has enlarged joints. Few dwarf wolves ever reach maturity, and virtually none are successful enough to reproduce.

Human intervention, however, changed that for dogs. Through human intervention, individuals that would never have become successful breeders passed on their genetic predisposition for the unusual. This same human attitude towards the unusual exists today. Just look at late twentieth-century breeding of cats that has perpetuated dwarfism in the Munchkin breed, or hairlessness in the Sphynx breed.

Similarly, the ancient Chinese or their trading partners actively bred accidental dwarf to accidental dwarf, producing a line of dogs that perpetuated this physical change. Over 5,000 years ago, dwarf breeds of dogs already existed in the royal dog kennels of China, probably just for their curiosity value, but eventually breeders realized that dwarfs might actually be useful.

Breeders in ancient Persia saw that dwarf dogs, although no longer fleet-footed, could be bred for enhanced scent-following ability. The advantage of these dogs over those with natural-length legs was that hunters could keep up with them more easily as they followed scent trails. Careful breeding initially took place in ancient Persia, an important centre of early breeding advances, but reached its most sophisticated level in medieval Europe.

Swift, fleet-footed dogs were introduced into Europe from Asia at least 3,000 years ago. They became the hunting companions of the nobility who hunted on horseback. By adding dwarf genes to these hunting hounds, a great variety of breeds now called bassets became hunting companions of those who hunted on foot.

With the decline of hunting and the advent of breed clubs, selective breeding moved away from practicality and over to extremes. The longest back, largest head or shortest legs became breeder's objectives. In the last one hundred years, dwarf breeds have been bred for extremes, not for utility. This is why painful arthritis became a serious canine problem in the twentieth century, and it will continue to be a potential problem for all dwarf breeds. It can be diminished though selective breeding to lengthen legs and shorten backs.

Giant dogs

Although natural selection favoured dogs smaller than wolves, and human intervention in breeding further diminished the wolf-dog's size (so that it was less dangerous in the human settlement), the animal still retained the genetic potential to return to the size of its founding parents. Under ideal circumstances, it could grow even larger than its wolf ancestors.

Once the wolf's more problematic behaviours of fearfulness, wariness, prudence and circumspection had all been diminished – in essence, once the wolf had become the dog – breeders were free to add size to their creation. This produced an intimidating weapon. The aggressive giant dog might have a shortened life expectancy, but under human control it was certainly an effective and impressive weapon.

Some of these giant dogs also had a natural inclination to be proprietorial: to protect their turf. If they were raised with livestock (goats and sheep), then they protected them from wolves as if the flock were members of the dog's own pack. Big got results.

The colour of certain giant breeds was carefully chosen by people; it was not a matter of chance. From the Caucasus Mountains of Asia, through Turkish Anatolia, the Balkans, the Carpathian Mountains, the Alps, the Pyrenees – even into west Africa – there are breeds of giant white dogs. People selected these colours not for aesthetic reasons but for practical considerations. A white dog blends into the flock of white sheep it is protecting. It's only when a wolf gets too close that this giant 'sheep' shows its magnificent size and says, 'I ain't no sheep.'

The thick, dense coat of these giants – the Caucasian Ovtcharkas, Turkish Akbash, Hungarian Kommondor, Polish Tatra Mountain Sheepdog, Slovakian Kuvasz, Italian Maremma, Spanish Pyrenean Mastiff and even the Aidi of the Moroccan Atlas Mountains – also had a practical purpose. In fights with wolves, the coat protected the skin from wounds. The distribution of these massive white dogs leaves a living reminder of thousand-year-old trails of human migration, trade or invasion from Asia through Europe.

'It won't work. You're an attack dog,
I'm a comfort dog…'

Hairless dogs

Hairlessness is uncommon, but it is not exactly a rare genetic 'mistake'. One of the dogs I was raised with, a Yorkshire terrier with a fine and luxurious coat, gave birth to a pup we called Misty, who had long blond hair on the crown of her head and feathering on her legs but was otherwise bald. The Chinese, as always in the vanguard of selective breeding, were probably the first to realize the value of ancient Mistys as mobile hot-water bottles.

Other hairless breeds either were selectively developed in Africa or reached there from Asia. When Europeans discovered the Americas, they came across hairless dogs high in the Peruvian mountains, bred by the Incas to provide night-time warmth. These dogs were either bred from Asian dogs brought to North America in the original migration of people from Asia into North America; were brought to Peru by unknown Polynesian or African people who arrived there before Europeans; or were the result of spontaneous genetic mutations as happened with Misty. (The Mexican hairless dog may be indigenous, or it may be a descendant of hairless African dogs brought to Mexico by the Spaniards.)

Regardless of its origin, hairlessness can only be perpetuated by very careful breeding of hairless individuals to others that have coats. Some of the descendants are coated and some are not. Both must be used in future breeding in order to keep hairlessness 'alive'.

'I'm getting a woolly cardigan
for Christmas!'

Breeding today and in the future

By encouraging the dog's evolution from the wolf, then altering the wolf-dog into two-pound Chihuahuas and 200-pound mastiffs, people carried out the most spectacular genetic manipulation ever achieved. Breeders accentuated some wolf behaviours and diminished others: a dramatic genetic manipulation carried out by trail and error. In the process, there were countless combinations that didn't function as breeders planned, and these were discarded.

Almost everywhere today, selective breeding involves only pure-bred dogs. There is, however, a magnificent advantage in retaining the large pool of mutts, mongrels, Heinzes, bitzers, random-breds – call them what you like. This is the most delicious genetic soup, a *mélange* that can be dipped into at any time to add a little spice to the restricted genetic pool within a specific breed.

Throughout the history of the dog, this genetic pool has remained constant. Last century saw the advent of intensified selective breeding and the creation of hundreds of written 'breed standards'.

Some of these breeds descended from restricted gene-pools. For example, all bearded collies descend from a specific mating of two dogs in the mid-1940s. Virtually all Nova Scotia Duck Tolling retrievers, more popular in Sweden than in their native Canada, descend from similar narrow bloodlines. If there are 'bad' genes in the parent stock, all the descendants carry these genes, embedding the defects permanently in the breed. If we were to reduce the dog's genetic pool to the 400 or so breeds recognized today, the genetic soup from which improvements come would become very thin and watery.

There is another problem on the horizon. Today, understanding how genes control not just size and colour but also susceptibility to disease and even temperament means that what once was carried out by trial and error can now be conducted more accurately. For example, science has discovered that a specific gene is responsible for a certain form of blindness in Irish setters, a blindness caused by progressive retinal atrophy, or 'PRA'.

In its simplest form, genetic manipulation means genetic testing and avoidance of breeding – for instance, from Irish setters that carry the dangerous PRA gene. Most people accept this concept. In a more controversial form, though, genetic manipulation means snipping out this dangerous gene from an Irish setter's germ cells, its eggs or sperm, and splicing in a 'safe' gene from another dog without a genetic predisposition to PRA. Many people feel this is not an ethically acceptable scientific activity. I disagree. To my mind this is simply a faster method of doing what dog breeders have been doing by trial and error for centuries.

There is, however, a completely different concept of genetic manipulation that involves splicing genes from one species into another. This has been done, for example, to make a mouse's nails glow in the dark. This form of genetic manipulation is profoundly different to the accelerated improvement of a species that can be achieved by replacing 'bad' genes with 'good' ones from the same species, and is an ethical problem we must confront now.

'Sorry, I don't do sticks. Try steaks.'

chapter two

HOW DOGS THINK AND LEARN

Most of the 400-plus breeds throughout the world were developed for utilitarian reasons: to guard, attack, herd, chase, fight, kill, follow scent trails, point, set, retrieve, pull carts or sleds, turn spits, or simply to comfort. How has a single species become so modified from its genetic origins, with so many groups or families within that species which have such varied and very specific purposes?

I'll get back to practical aspects of breed differences in behaviour, but first I want to touch briefly on a little theory about how dogs think and learn. Recent developments in the study of human behaviour give some clues to the dog's potential to understand, comprehend and learn. It is now widely accepted in scientific circles that human language is an instinct. Steven Pinker's fascinating book, *The Language Instinct*, describes how all people, regardless of who we are, where we live or what language we speak, use nouns, verbs, adjectives and all aspects of language in similar ways. (The most recent genetic evidence, published since Pinker wrote his book, suggests that our ability to use language evolved as a result of genetic shifts in humans around 200,000 years ago.) We learn a language through experience and training, but the *ability* to learn language is hard-wired into our brains. Learning language is simply one of the many inherent learning facilities we are born with.

Learning language uses a different part of the brain than the part involved in learning, for example, trigonometry or an appreciation of aesthetics. There are many different learning centres in the brain and, most importantly, there is no such thing as a single 'learning centre'. This concept has led to changes in our attitude to learning. Within (human) social sciences, a new model of human behaviour integrates both psychology and anthropology into the natural sciences, especially into neuroscience and evolutionary biology. This new integrated field, known as 'Evolutionary Psychology', looks at aspects of mental life we take for granted, such as perceiving, reasoning and acting, and says that each of these activities requires its own well-engineered software.

There are many different learning mechanisms for different spheres of experience, and in dogs, as in us, they sometimes work at cross purposes. Learning is not accomplished by a single, general-purpose learning centre. Like us, dogs are flexible because their minds contain different modules, each with provisions to learn in its own way. Selective breeding reinforces some of these modules more than others, creating more efficient learning mechanisms for some activities in some breeds and other equally efficient learning methods for other activities in other breeds. All of these hard-wired biological systems evolved to help the wolf survive and reproduce. Via selective breeding, we've accentuated some systems and diminished others.

What differentiates humans from dogs is the influence of culture. In human culture, behaviour spreads from person to person, almost like a contagion. Remember how wearing backwards baseball caps spread within months, like a cultural virus, into every human nook and cranny in the world? Other than in puppyhood, dogs are relatively poor learners from the examples of others dogs. In that sense, they have more limited 'cultural' influences.

'She's being a bitch.
I put it down to PMT.'

What dogs have learning centres for

I think dogs have hard-wired individual learning centres for the following.

•Intuitive knowledge of motions and forces; understanding mechanics: *That branch is going to fall on me.*

•Mental mapping of large territories: *I recognize that route. I've been here before and know my way home.*

•Habitat selection, for safety and productivity: *No one can get at me if I eat this bone under this bed.*

•Patrolling, investigating and marking territory: *I must check out and mark this property.*

•Understanding dangers, including caution, fear, phobias: *I won't walk across that plank.*

•Food, including intuitive biology – what is good to eat: *I'll eat this but not that.*

•Intuitive understanding of other animals' behaviour; predicting their behaviour from their actions: *I'll chase this small one but not that large one.*

•Relationships, both kinship and dominance: *I'll let my pup do that to me but I won't let anyone else.*

•Mating, including differences in sexual attraction: *I know who's who and which end is which.*

Each individual dog inherits hard-wired modules for all of these specific types of behaviour, but in some breeds, modules for certain behaviours are more efficiently wired than in others. (For example, the learning centre for what is good to eat is so inefficiently wired in Labradors that they'll eat anything!) All breeds share common behaviours, but through selective breeding for specific behaviours within individual breeds, some behaviours have been intensified, while others have been diminished.

In the last half of the last century, one of the most dramatic changes in the evolution of the dog took place. In an extraordinarily short period of time, the utilitarian role of the majority of dog breeds ended and was replaced with new responsibilities: aesthetic appeal and companionship.

Today, in veterinary practice, I see a diversity of dogs bred to conform to the physical attributes of breed type as written into kennel club morphological breed standards, but few of these individuals are bred today for their original utility or for function. Even within the small population of dogs that are bred for utility rather than conformation, most are also kept for companionship.

Most Labradors have joint problems, but I have a secret stash!

Our perception of the modern dog

In Europe, North America, Australasia and Japan, the dog is treated as a member of the family rather than as a possession or an object of simple material value. According to an American Animal Hospital Association survey:

- •69% of owners spend at least forty-five minutes per day in dog-related activities;

- •59% of owners permit their dogs to sleep in their bedrooms;

- •54% of owners say they are emotionally attached to their dogs;

- •57% of owners would want a pet as their only companion if deserted on an island;

- •79% give their pets holiday and birthday gifts;

- •62% of pet owners often sign letters or cards from themselves and their pets;

•55% of pet owners consider themselves to be 'mom' and 'dad' to their pets;

•33% talk to their pets through the telephone or the answering machine.

This change in our perception of the dog is beginning to be reflected in law. The law classifies dogs as property or 'chattels', and when compensation for the loss of a dog is required, this is based on the cost of purchasing a replacement.

Beginning in the 1970s, courts in many countries began to make awards based not only upon the replacement value of a pet, but also for any non-economic losses such as 'emotional distress' or 'loss of companionship'. Increasingly in the US, states are rewriting their laws to state explicitly that a family dog has a value beyond that of a chattel: that it has emotional as well as property value, and compensation for any loss must include this additional value.

For example, in New Jersey, up to $20,000 damages can be awarded for the 'loss of companionship' of a dog. In Massachusetts, damages can be awarded 'for loss of the reasonably expected society, companionship, comfort, protection and services of the deceased animal to his or her human companions'. Pet trusts, which allow money to be left to animals, are now legal in eighteen American states, meaning that pets can be 'heirs'.

Here's the biggest change: in some states, the status of a 'dog owner' is changing to that of the dog's 'guardian'. A dog's guardian can sue in court on a dog's behalf, with any damages awarded payable into a trust set up to provide care for the rest of the dog's life.

Sex differences in behaviour

In dogs in general, behaviours such as nervousness, excitability, destructiveness, trainability, barking and playfulness are enhanced or diminished through selective breeding. There are also sex differences in some of these dog behaviours.

Fairly consistently, female dogs are easier to obedience-train, easier to house-train and demand more affection, while male dogs are more likely to be aggressive with other dogs, act in a dominant

'Smutt is a sweet, gentle dog. Wish I
could say the same for his missus.'

manner and be active, or even destructive. Male dogs are only slightly more likely to snap at children. (There are no appreciable sex differences in watchdog barking, excitability or playfulness.)

However, sex differences in certain behaviours also vary from breed to breed. For example, while in the dog population in general, males are only slightly more likely to snap at children, and German shepherds, for example, conform to the canine average, male golden retrievers and male cocker spaniels are more likely than the average male dog to snap at children, while male Labradors are less likely than the average male dog to do so. In toy poodles, breeders report the female to be less reliable with children than the male.

Coat colour and temperament are related

I mentioned Russian studies in fox breeding (page 16). This took place because the fur market was moving from natural red fox fur to a demand for silver fox fur. What unexpectedly happened was that by selectively breeding for silver, the foxes became more tame within only seven generations. Other morphological and behavioural changes occurred. The silver foxes had smaller brains, barked more, wanted to sit on laps and sought out human company. Some fox cubs had drooping ears. Black and white piebald coats appeared. Even a twice-yearly breeding cycle developed.

In dogs there are now several published reports on temperament differences also associated with colour, especially in the English cocker spaniel. Several years ago I carried out a survey of 1,100 professional dog breeders, asking them to answer questions about behaviour within the breed they bred, according to coat colour. Standard poodle breeders, for example, reported no significant differences by coat colour in the poodle's enjoyment in being petted, anxious or protective barking, excitability, aggressiveness to strangers entering its home or likelihood of snapping at unknown children. They did, however, report that black poodles are easier to house-train and most unlikely to disobey, while apricot poodles are more difficult to house-train and more likely to disobey. These experienced breeders (exhibiting at Crufts Dog Show in Birmingham, England) also reported that black poodles are most willing to play with other dogs, whites are also more playful than average, but apricots and browns are less likely to initiate play. They said black standard poodles are better than average at responding to obedience training, browns and whites are typical for the breed, but apricots require a little more patience on the part of the trainer.

The typical standard poodle is more at ease meeting strangers than most other breeds, but while whites, blacks and browns are typical, apricots are somewhat less sure of themselves. Standard poodles seldom whine for attention, but within the breed, while browns and whites are average, blacks are less likely to grizzle and moan, and apricots are more likely to use their voices to gain the attention of their owners. As a breed, standard

'Is that breeding or what?'

poodles are less destructive at home than almost any other breed, but within the breed, while whites are about average, blacks are less likely to chew furniture and scratch wallpaper; browns and especially apricots are more likely to do so. Poodles thrive on physical activity, but once again, there are subtle differences according to coat colour. While apricots and whites demand slightly less physical activity than average, browns and especially blacks need more.

Differences in behaviour according to coat colour were reported in the other breeds I surveyed. For example, yellow Labradors are more excitable, destructive and disobedient, less reliable with children (although still exceptionally reliable) and bark more than black Labradors. Yellow Labradors are reported as better house guards. Black German shepherds enjoy being petted more, are more reliable with children and are more playful with other dogs than white German shepherds. White shepherds are more disobedient, nervous and wary of strangers on their territory than are black shepherds.

Coat type and behaviour may be linked

Surprisingly, coat length within a breed may also be related to behaviour. For example, breeders feel that smooth-haired dachshunds are more likely to be disobedient than their wire-haired or long-haired relatives. While long-haired and wire-haired dachshunds are slightly better than average when confronted with an unknown five-year-old child on their own territory, the smooth-haired are less reliable than average. This difference is behaviour also applies to the acceptance of strange adults in the dog's home. Smoothies accept strangers less willingly than others. Long- and wire-haired dachshunds are significantly less nervous than smooth hairs. Remember, this applies to dog populations in general.

Problems with breeding for looks

As a practising clinical veterinarian, my biggest concern over what we've done wrong in breeding dogs for their looks is how this has affected their health and their life expectancy. Inherited disease is endemic in individual breeds.

Mention cavalier King Charles spaniels and a vet thinks 'heart disease'. The word 'Dobermann' brings to mind auto-immune conditions, including auto-immune heart disease. West Highland white terriers have skin allergies. Labradors have joint problems. Virtually every breed suffers from problems that were unwittingly accentuated through selective breeding. The Irish wolfhound, Rottweiler, Afghan hound and Weimaraner are more likely to die from cancer than the average dog. The Irish wolfhound, bulldog, and Bernese mountain dog all have a median life expectancy over forty percent shorter than the average dog.

Selective breeding can also be life-enhancing. Beagles, cavalier King Charles spaniels, dachshunds and Irish setters are less likely to die from cancer than the average dog, while miniature poodles, miniature dachshunds, Bedlington terriers and whippets typically live lives that are twenty percent longer than the average dog.

'Handsome – yes.
But cement for brains.'

Breeds can remain – behaviour can be changed

According to geneticists, in humans, eighty-five percent of genetic variation consists of differences between one person and another within the same ethnic group. Another eight percent of genetic variation occurs among ethnic groups, and seven percent among races. In other words, the genetic differences between two randomly picked Japanese is about twelve times as large as the genetic difference between the average for all Japanese and the average, for example, for all Icelanders.

Surprisingly, the most recent canine genetic studies show there are greater genetic differences between dog breeds than between different human races. Differences between dog breeds account for as much as thirty percent of genetic variation. In addition, variation within many breeds, especially those that are the most popular and numerous, is still enormous.

We can alter and modify a breed by selecting for behaviour as well as looks. I watched that happen in the 1970s and '80s, when Pyrenean mountain dog breeders successfully reduced the inherent predatory aggression that existed in their dogs, producing the more reliable family companions of today. Selective breeding carried out intelligently not only reduces the incidence of inherited diseases, it can have positive effects on the way a dog thinks and learns.

'Don't be like that;
I'm *bred* to wear silly hats!'

'Any room for me on there, old chap?'

chapter three
HOW DOGS INFLUENCE
YOUR BEHAVIOUR

Fat, lazy, aggressive, timid, good-looking, ugly… all of these physical and behavioural characteristics of dogs can, and do, influence your behaviour towards them. Some of these characteristics exist *because* of your behaviour. There are powerful, hidden psychological reasons why we behave the way we do with our dogs.

The modern dog is, in a curious way, a human artifact. Those people who originally selectively bred wolves and created dogs, bred for practical purposes: trainability, speed and barking. Curiously, they also selectively bred for larger frontal sinuses on wolves' heads – an anatomical feature of no apparent practical or utilitarian value. They didn't know it, but they were instinctively breeding wolves both to look more intelligent and to look more juvenile.

A powerful human instinct draws people to the shapes and behaviours of young animals. In one of his most famous articles, ethnologist Konrad Lorenz explained that the differences in form between babies and adults triggers different responses in people. 'Baby' shapes – large eyes, bulging craniums (or, anatomically speaking, enlarged frontal sinuses) and small chins – trigger the release in us of an automatic surge of disarming tenderness.

From the very earliest intervention in their breeding, dogs have been selectively bred to look more 'juvenile' than their forebears. Science calls this process 'neoteny'. Not only that, people selectively bred dogs to behave in a juvenile way. Their dependent behaviour has been most exaggerated in the last two hundred years. Crying, smiling, following, scrambling, clinging, lifting the arms or clapping the hands in greeting and approaching – all of these are human infant behaviours that instinctively stimulate a nurturing response from us adults.

I wish I had the money
for liposuction…

Dogs, juvenile or adult, exhibit many of these behaviours, too. The naturalist Gerald Durrell called 'smiling' the dog's trump card. I agree. I took hundreds of pictures of my dog Macy when we took a two-month trip across America. I rotate these pictures as screensavers on my computer and in every single one she's 'smiling'.

Breeding turned the wolf into a life-long wolf cub. Although they are chronologically adults, dogs remain both mentally and physically forever infantile, an evolutionary development on their part that triggered an instinctive caring and nurturing response from people. If we have children, they, too, trigger a nurturing response from us – but our kids grow up. In a sense, dogs are super-abundant child substitutes: unchanging, constant, forever cute and sweet in a dependent, baby way.

People find it almost impossible to avoid using human terms to describe dog behaviour. A degree of 'anthropomorphism' – attributing human feelings and emotions to other animals – is inescapable. Only the remaining, antiquated 'cause and effect' scientists from an older and more rigid scientific tradition feel uncomfortable with it. It is a profound and positive component part of the relationship we have with our pets, but it is also an undercurrent in our fantasies about pets.

As far as I'm concerned, a level of anthropomorphism is perfectly acceptable – but there are limits. Czech writer Karel Ciapek was reasonable in his assumptions when he wrote, 'If dogs could talk, perhaps we would find it as hard to get along with them as we do with people.'

Ciapek lived with dachshunds – which might explain his pragmatic attitude.

A mutually beneficial relationship

Dogs are givers and receivers. In that sense you could say that dogs are 'symbiotic parasites', because they satisfy some of our instinctive needs while at the same time gaining in so many ways from their association with us. We instinctively feel safe in the presence of other animals with superior senses and have learned through experience that dogs are genuinely good to have at our feet.

Although some dogs seem to have travelled a greater distance from their wolf origins, we still think that our own dogs, regardless of their shape or size, will defend and protect us, just as a member of a wolf pack will come to the aid of another member when it's attacked. There's a grain of truth in this idea, but there are more complicated and hidden reasons why we think our dogs will protect us, and this is at the root of how they influence the way we behave with them.

Strange as it seems, although outwardly dogs are like human children, dependent on their owners for food, security and good health, in a curious way

'Tuesday at 4.30 any good for you?'

there is a reversal in the relationship. Subconsciously, the relationship flips. In a curious and subliminal way, dogs become our 'parents' and we become their dependents.

When a child is born, it depends so completely on its mother that, for the first year or more of life, it doesn't even consider itself to be independent from her; the human baby is 'merged' with mother. Mother provides warmth, nourishment and protection. When the baby touches its mother, the baby's sense of arousal diminishes. It becomes calm. Its heart rate slows, its skin temperature drops, its blood pressure returns to normal. Mother means contentment and security.

A little later in life, the baby enters the first stage of true independence and begins to realize that it is a unique being. This is the beginning of separation from mother. Some people call this stage the 'terrible twos', because it often leads to frustration: tantrums and crying. The feeling of security that mother provides remains, but it becomes altered by the realities of life.

In a curious way, a dog provides some of the instinctive comforts that mother once did, and these are based on touch. If you stroke a dog you don't know, your blood pressure and heart rate rise. But if you stroke your own dog, your blood pressure, skin temperature and heart rate drop. Your state of arousal diminishes. This happens only when a social relationship has developed between the stroker and the dog.

Petting and stroking the soft, warm fur of your own dog stimulates the same physiological response that you once had as a baby when you touched your mother. In this context, psychologists call dogs 'transitional objects', because they provide warmth and security in the same way that teddy bears and security blankets do. Subconsciously, the dog offers the same feeling of security that mother did during the first eighteen months of life. Perfectly sensible people feel that their dogs will defend and protect them because, in the hidden subconscious life of the owner, the dog is the all-powerful and protective parent.

When my daughter Tamara first brought her Labrador pup Lola to our house, my dog Macy gathered around her all her soft toys and prevented Lola from playing with them. This is a normal canine behaviour, but we interpreted Macy's behaviour as 'selfishness', a human trait we're all familiar with. By doing so, unconsciously we made Macy in our minds a little less 'animal' and a little more human. We're wrong. Her behaviour should remind us that our behaviours are not uniquely human; we share them with many other species.

People with dogs have the stimulating and exciting privilege of being front-row observers of how a completely distinct species thinks and behaves. Sometimes we forget that dogs are just as 'animal' as any other species. The fact that we happen to share a wide range of feelings, emotions and behaviours with dogs should not make them any less animal that their wild cousins. Rather, it should make us appreciate that a great range of animals share with us feelings, emotions and attitudes that are thought by some to be uniquely human.

'My share portfolio has gone through the floor, Boris, but you're the only one who understands…'

We've become hooked on dogs

There was a time, only a few generations ago, when a dog was allowed to lead a dog's life. In the countryside, suburbia and small towns, many dogs lived in doghouses in the garden or, if allowed in the house, were restricted to the kitchen. Dogs wandered off to do what dogs wanted to do: sniff lampposts, roll in or eat horse dung. This is still what most dogs would really like to do. As a child, I took it as normal that Angus, our Scottie, spent the day outdoors and that his daily activities included at least one visit to the local delicatessen for a tasty handout.

Where I lived in Toronto, in what is now a bygone era, unneutered males would get together in a benign 'brotherhood' and hang out at the home of the resident bitch in season. This 'pack' never acted as a genuine pack: hunting and eating together. Each gang member returned home each evening for food and warmth, joining up with other members the following day to do a little scavenging, to sniff more lampposts and to look for bitches. Life had few hang-ups. Dogs had few behaviour problems because they were allowed to act like dogs.

But society has changed. A major change was the replacement of horse power by car power. Naturally, this increased the dog's risk of road-traffic accidents but more importantly, it dramatically reduced the amount of horse manure on the streets. Suddenly, dog droppings, a previously mild and inconsequential environmental inconvenience, became a social nuisance. In the absence of other excrement, dog droppings now shone bright on the landscape.

At the same time, dogs were invited to live in people's homes, initially to live in the kitchen and occupy other floor space, but then, almost surreptitiously, to climb on sofas, even beds. Today, in North America and western Europe, surveys report that about half of all pet dogs are allowed on their owners' beds. The smaller the dog, the more likely it is to sleep with people.

This increasing intimacy has brought with it a greater feeling of attachment and responsibility on the part of owners. Conscientious owners feel a responsibility to their neighbours and try to control their dogs' outdoor activities. More important is our emotional need to protect our dogs. That is why we keep our canine companions in luxurious 'jails' for most of their lives: locked in our homes. We think that by feeding the best food and by providing creature comforts – warmth, soft bedding and chewy toys – that dogs have landed feet first in heaven. We forget that these are but physical comforts.

I am not advocating total freedom for dogs. Dogs have never been 'free'; the actual concept of 'dog' denies it. The dog is our creation, bred under our control for our own purposes. What happened in the twentieth century is that, as we developed stronger emotional attachments to our dogs, former limited canine freedoms were eliminated and replaced by what we consider to be physical luxuries. As our emotional dependency on dogs increased, their limited freedoms were further eroded. This may be one of the reasons why canine behaviour problems have increased in the last few decades.

'I don't give a stuff *who* you go
out with! You really must stop
anthropomorphizing me!'

Dogs and children

Although we treat our dogs as 'kids', as parents we often get dogs for our children's 'amusement'. After all, if our kids play with the dog, we have more time to get on with other chores. However, it is very likely that, although we don't consciously acknowledge the fact, we're saying something important to our children when we bring a dog into the home with this attitude. In this sense, dogs are not simply childhood amusements.

Sensible parents tell their children that they're responsible for their dog. Yet unless a child is emotionally very mature, this is simply not true. Parents are responsible for the physical and emotional well-being of family dogs. However, this standard parental proclamation of responsibility is often the first intimation children have of their responsibility for living things. When a parent introduces a dog into the home and says, 'It's for the children,' what he or she is really saying is, 'I think parenting is important and I want my child to start parenting now.' In all cultures, from wealthy and sophisticated to primitive and basic, women and children are responsible for pets. In hunter/gatherer societies, children learn about animal behaviour at least in part through pets. In our society, they have an early opportunity to learn about their later responsibilities to the living world around them.

Hidden rewards from your dog

Dogs are unambiguous compared to people; what you see is what you get. Dogs may be speechless, but they are perfect communicators. Well over eighty percent of dog owners feel their dogs understand their feelings and emotions.

This curious fact was lucidly examined among deaf people in Britain who acquired 'hearing dogs' to act as their ears, to tell them there is a knock on the door, a smoke alarm has gone off or the baby is crying – sounds that the hearing world takes for granted. In a study that lasted several years, investigators observed that feelings of self-esteem, self-reliance and personal worth dramatically increased in people who acquired 'hearing dogs'. I've been involved with the charity Hearing Dogs for Deaf People since the early 1980s, and these improvements were far in excess of what had been expected from dogs acting simply as sensory aids, or 'ears' for deaf people.

When the investigators studied these changes in more detail, they observed that the deaf people and their dogs were actually communicating mutely with each other – or at least the people felt they were. Words or any other noises were not exchanged; communication took place through body language. The deaf people felt that their dogs understood how they felt emotionally, without the need to explain. They felt their dogs understood better than people did – that with people they needed to explain things verbally, but with dogs they did not. And because these people had living beings in their homes that

'How hard would it be to smile?'

understood their feelings and emotions, their feelings of self-worth and confidence improved.

If this is the experience of deaf people, it's very likely that hearing people experience similar emotional benefits just by saying, 'Isn't life rough, Spot?' and feeling that Spot doesn't have to respond. Spot seemingly deeply understands, and there's no need for him to respond. This is mute understanding at its purest.

In reality, it may be that Spot hasn't got an inkling of the emotional turmoil his owner has, but that doesn't matter. His owner feels that Spot understands, and that's what's most important.

A major branch of modern psychiatry is called 'non-interventive'. The psychiatrist listens. This form of psychiatry is in many ways similar to the non-judgemental, non-interventive approach dogs have to their owner's problems. If it really works, it's not only easier to talk to dogs, it is astoundingly cheaper and available twenty-four hours a day, without appointment.

Our attitude to different dog looks

Pure-bred dogs, bred for coat colour, length and texture, and for body shape and size, may have been bred initially for practical purposes, but today they are almost universally bred for 'good looks'. Physical attributes, such as a thick or wiry coat to protect the dog from the elements, are now selectively enhanced to appeal to people's eyes and sense of touch.

Really good-looking dogs can literally 'get away with murder' because of another human idiosyncrasy. Curiously, people don't particularly like absolute perfection in other people – or in dogs. They prefer perfection tinged with a little human weakness, or in the case of dogs, a reversion to canine instincts.

In one fascinating scientific study, an American psychologist had actors answer an educational quiz. Several actors were asked to answer questions equally correctly, but one of these actors was asked to make a noisy commotion, then say, in an anguished tone, 'Oh my goodness, I've spilled coffee all over my suit.' That was the person the listeners to tapes of the conversations found most attractive.

My seductively gorgeous golden retriever is admired for her aesthetic beauty. But when she chased and killed a rabbit, although I was angry and distressed, there was also a deep-seated feeling of admiration that such a pretty dog could still behave like a dog. If an ugly dog were to commit the same crime, I'm sure it would get far less human consideration.

'They say dogs tend to look like their owners...'

'...or is it the other way around?'

Extensions of our own personalities

Dogs play several roles in our lives. One of them is to act as an extension of the owner's personality. We like to project our own sexual image of ourselves through the clothes we wear, and dogs are, to some extent, accessories to that image. This is why, historically, men generally prefer either lean, muscular, short-coated dogs or working breeds while women may select these shapes but also choose more cuddly varieties like Bichon Frises, Shih Tzus and Pekingese. There is still among men a class distinction in their choice of dogs. Working-class men still prefer guarding breeds like German shepherds, Dobermanns and Rottweilers. If they must have a medium-sized dog, it's a muscular bull terrier variety: a Staffordshire, English or pit bull terrier. If a small dog is forced upon them, they prefer small, hard, 'teeth-and-muscles' dogs like Jack Russell terriers.

Middle-class man is different. He's usually university educated and is aware of his female as well as his male side. If he's confident in his sexual identity, then he's quite happy to be seen in public walking a ball of fluff and may even take pride in the fact that he's seen in public with what is still, to many people, a feminine image. Of course, some men have no say in what the family dog looks like. In these circumstances, basic man might want a masculine-image dog but find himself lumbered with a Chihuahua. He'll be much less embarrassed to walk this dog if the dog, small as it is, has a deep blood-lust and tries to attack anything living.

We have ambivalent feelings about dogs. In one sense the pet dog is a true family member. It is fed, housed and cared for like other family members. It participates in family activities, from watching television to walking in parks to family vacations. We come to see our dogs as individuals, different from all others, even from others of the same breed.

Those of us who live with dogs eventually treat them as unique and irreplaceable individuals. We worry when our dogs are unwell and mourn when they die. Our inconsistency in our emotional attitude towards dogs is still based on the prevailing feeling that the human is a distinct and unique species, separate from all others. This is a relic-like attitude left over from cultural history. Changes are gradually taking place, and the feeling of domination and control over all animals, including dogs, is being eroded and replaced by a feeling of responsibility for other animals. In the near future, however, dogs will continue to lead threatened lives: loved one day, abandoned the next.

Why dogs are happy to be fat

Veterinarians estimate that at least a third of all dogs are clinically overweight. Pet-food manufacturers know this makes an excellent market, and have responded by producing a range of low-calorie tinned and dry foods, even low-calorie snacks, usually called 'light' – as if a feathery name vaporizes fat.

Fat dogs are a human creation, and their perpetuation lies in the hidden role dogs play in our lives. In any family with an overweight canine, the dog has discovered the soft touch: the person most likely to give treats. More often than not, this is a male, usually the family breadwinner. The dog learns that, while the family's woman and children follow the vet's instructions to cut calories and increase activities, the dominant male is, curiously, the weak link. He gives extra food because he finds it difficult to show his emotions, to be physical, to touch. With his children, he expresses affection by giving them money, so with his dog he offers pretzels and cookies. Dogs quickly recognize these people and manipulate them. Dogs are fat simply because we overfeed them.

'It's *your* fault we're fat.'

Your dog says something about you

It's a common adage that we look like our dogs. The question is: 'cause or effect'? Do dogs end up looking like their owners, or do we choose dogs that already look like us? There's no doubt that the type of dog we have says something about us, but psychologists who have interviewed dog owners say that what we live with reveals aspects of our individual personalities.

The American Kennel Club classifies all dogs into seven groups: toys, terriers, hounds (sight and scent hunters), herders (livestock drivers and pro- tectors), workers (large guarding breeds), sporting dogs (gun dogs) and non-sporting dogs (anything left over). In a study of American dog owners, toy-breed owners are the most nurturing and least dominant. Terrier owners are the least aggressive but most dependent on others for emotional support. Hound people are the friendliest; herding-breed owners are the most aggressive and orderly; and working-breed people are the most dominant dog owners. Sporting-breed owners are the wealthiest. Non-sporting-breed owners are a mixed bag.

Whatever your dog says about you, regardless of whether you subconsciously chose it as an extension of your personality or to fill a void in your emotional life, your dog will come to influence your behaviour. That influence can be to its own detriment when it interferes with your willingness or capability to train your canine buddy.

'I chew up everything except my
food, which I swallow whole.'

chapter four
HOW TO CONTROL
WHAT YOUR DOG DOES

The better you integrate your dog into your human family, the more fruitful and satisfying your mutual relationship is. This is the simple aim of dog training. To be successful, it's best to first understand how your dog thinks, how she interprets your tone of voice, your body language, your use of rewards and discipline, even your timing. It's easy to control what she does. If you set up the wrong house rules or are inconsistent with your approach to your dog, however, you create problems that can be difficult to undo. Spend time understanding why your dog does what he or she does and how you should interact with your canine. Don't forge ahead with dog training that may inadvertently create problems which later need to be 'unlearned'.

Although many of the dogs I see each day have been neutered, I still think of them as males and females. I don't like calling a dog 'it', and in the following, rather than constantly saying 'he or she', for convenience I'm going to refer to one sex only; as my own dogs are females, that's the sex I'll use. Of course, all that follows applies to both sexes.

'I've got fleas.'

'Ooh! Can I have some?'

The stages of life and of learning

Any dog is trainable, but the younger she is, the easier it will be. Young dogs are unwritten books. You control her early learning; by letting her explore new situations and by protecting her from developing unwarranted fears, her confidence develops. If you want her to be sure of herself in the presence of all types of people, introduce her early in life, indoors and out, to as wide a variety of experiences as possible: toddlers, older children, people with canes or walkers, in uniforms or wearing hats or motorcycle helmets, mothers with kids in buggies, people of different colours. The more she takes in, the less likely it is that she'll develop idiosyncratic fears or phobias.

Your dog's ability to learn alters as she grows through well-defined stages of development. All dogs go through these stages, but the speed of progress varies from one individual to another. Don't expect more from your dog than she's capable of giving. A dog's personality is being formed even while she's still in the womb. It is further developed during the first three weeks of life, but the most critical make-or-break period is from roughly three to twelve weeks of age. Experiences during this period influence lifelong attitudes. Much of this time is spent with the breeder, but during that eight- to twelve-week period when you take over responsibility, your pup will show a deep, genuine desire to please you. At the same time she's working out her proper position in her new pack: your family. If you give the right signals now, she learns that all family members are pack leaders. Give the wrong signals and she'll quite naturally try to find a higher position in the household hierarchy.

Early 'socializing' to other people, dogs and animals in and outside the home is overwhelmingly important – but there's a problem. Young pups only have temporary protection, inherited from their mothers, against certain infectious diseases. This is boosted with puppy inoculations. Although some vaccine manufacturers produce vaccines that are completed at ten weeks, there's still a two-week interval, finishing at twelve weeks, before a pup can safely meet other dogs. Your veterinarian understands the disease risk in your area. What I suggest is that, subject to your vet's approval, you take your pup out as soon as you get her, under controlled circumstances, and let her visit safe places. This means with friends' healthy dogs in their homes and gardens, in your car, on your lap in outdoor cafés or in other public areas where you know other dogs are routinely vaccinated. Good socializing early in life is probably the most important way to ensure good manners in adulthood.

'After you!'

From three to six months of age is comparable to our preteen years. At the beginning of this period a pup depends upon you and is still eager to please; by the end she's much more independent. Simple obedience training is easiest when your pup has the greatest desire to please: i.e. as soon as she moves in with you. Training becomes increasingly complicated as your pup develops a mind of her own.

In dogs, adolescence extends from six months to twelve to eighteen months. These are the teenage years, and just as with us they can be amusing, exasperating or downright irritating. Sexual maturity arrives quite some time before emotional maturity. Many dogs, but especially males, will challenge authority at some time during adolescence. Territorial behaviour also develops, in both males and females. This can be a difficult period. More dogs of this age are handed into dog shelters than of any other age. But if you lay down a firm foundation of good behaviour earlier in your dog's life, adolescent exuberance becomes only a temporary blip in relationships. Hold out. Adolescence does end!

Physical and sexual maturity are eventually followed by emotional maturity. This happy stage arrives at different times in different dogs and varies considerably according to breed. I am sure one of the reasons the golden retriever is so popular is because emotional maturity arrives early, shortly after a year of age. Boxers, on the other hand seem to go through the longest adolescence in dogdom! Emotional maturity may not develop until well over two or even three years of age in Boxer dogs.

How to communicate with dogs

From puppyhood, a dog uses the position of her tail, body and ears combined with eye contact and facial expression for communication. Voice is also used – barks, howls, growls and whines – but sound is much less important. Dogs are more acutely aware of body language than of voice. This is why pups learn to respond to hand signals so well.

Improve the way you communicate with your dog by using sensible body language accompanied by voice signals. For example, standing over your dog and looking straight down at her will be interpreted at a threat. On the other hand, getting down on your haunches (more at her level) and spreading your arms wide carries no threat but is an inviting gesture to come over. Most dogs will naturally respond by walking towards you. Training to vocal commands is then simple to introduce into activities.

As a pup willingly responds to welcoming body language she understands, say 'Come.' Soon she'll come to you at the mere sound of that word. Don't misinterpret your dog's body language. Staring at

'When they say "No", what they
really mean is "Yes".'

you may indicate interest but in certain circumstances it's a sign of dominance. Showing the teeth is usually a sign of canine dominance, but some dogs show their teeth in a greeting 'grin' – really a submissive sign of appeasement.

When using your voice, think about the sounds a dog naturally responds to. Wolves howl at night to locate each other. Dogs also howl to communicate. A singsong 'Ma…cy' (my personal 'howl') attracts my dog Macy's attention. If a pup does something wrong – bites her mother too hard, for example – mother responds with a growl. A low-pitched quick 'Macy!' with a deep inflection (like her mother's growl) communicates a wholly different meaning to my dog. If during puppy play Macy bit a litter mate too hard, her brother or sister yipped in pain, called it quits and stopped play. Do the same. Say 'Ouch!' in a sharp tone and walk away. Your pup will understand your inflection and your body language.

Dogs have better hearing than we do: four times more acute, the experts tell us. Dogs certainly hear at the high end of sound frequency, the ultrasonic end inaudible to us. This creates both disadvantages and advantages for dogs. A disadvantage is that some dogs are too sound-sensitive. They go on to develop fear of sounds such as distant thunder. The advantage, to us in dog training, is that most dogs respond quickly to simple sounds such as a whistle. Think about using a distinctive sound to catch your dog's attention during early training. Whistle training is easy; think shepherds and sheepdogs. With a whistle, you can control your dog at a great distance without developing laryngitis.

Your pup depends upon you completely for her safety and security. She'll learn about life both on her own and with your help. Think like a dog when preparing your home and garden for your new arrival. That means pretty much thinking like a child. If you understand the impetuosity and curiosity of the toddler, you have a pretty good idea of how a pup views life. Develop a benign but firm 'parental' control of your dog's behaviour. Channel natural energy in productive ways. Avoid potential dangers and most important, remember that it is easiest to put instructions on a blank page. Once a dog has learned to do something one way, you'll have to 'untrain' her before training again. Whatever she's doing, she's always learning. Avoid common dangers, especially during the most inquisitive stage of her life: her first year.

'It's a great toy, but it only
squeaks sometimes.'

How dogs learn

Any dog – puppy or adult, female or male, town or country – learns about life the same way: through trial and error. A dog inherits certain characteristics from her parents, but her own unique personality is formed by the successes and failures of life, especially her early experiences before she is three months old. There's really no difference in understanding (or training) a puppy or an adult dog, but there's one overwhelmingly useful fact that influences how a young dog or mature dog thinks and behaves. A puppy is still wet clay, ready to be moulded to the lifestyle you want for her. Older dogs have already experienced a variety of successes and failures. The older dog's personality has been set by these experiences. Training an older dog is harder than training a pup because it often means unlearning something, then learning again. If you understand why dogs behave the way they do, it's simple to understand what motivates your new friend's behaviour.

Dogs are a joy because they're so gregariously curious. As I write this, twenty-week-old Lola is a daily visitor. Lola is my daughter Tamara's pup, born to my son's Labrador Inca. Did Lola mind leaving her mother and litter? If she did, she didn't give us any hints. Her natural curiosity is so potent that the rewards of investigating a new environment outweighed the loss of her previous playmates.

Pups will investigate anything – but take care; natural curiosity may lead to unexpected and unpleasant experiences. Your responsibility is to channel curiosity. For example, we let Lola approach unknown dogs, but we hover to prevent her curiosity from provoking others. We want her to learn there are limits, but don't want her to develop fear of other dogs.

Smell may be a dog's most important sense but during puppyhood, taste reigns. Pups taste life. If a magazine or letter is on the floor, it'll be chewed. If you leave your coat over a kitchen chair, the hem will be chewed. Pups *must* chew, so it's up to you to provide appropriate chew toys. Remember that trial and error is the natural way dogs learn. You can shape and channel your dog's learning by planning ahead.

Prepare for learning

I like to think that our relationship with our own parents evolves from total dependency to mutual friendship. From the very beginning, your relationship with your dog should involve both of these characteristics: leadership and friendship. Dogs innately understand status. Make sure that, quite independent from formal training sessions, in all your relationships with your dog she understands by your actions and deeds that you are superior.

At the same time, if you want formal training to be fast, productive and fun for both of you, your dog should be relaxed – not apprehensive – in your company. Relaxed dogs learn faster. They appreciate your praise. They want to please you. Some people feel that old-fashioned punishment training – for example, pushing your dog's nose in its urine when it messes in the wrong place, choke-chains to control boisterousness – works. Yes, it can work, but at the expense of creating needless fear in your dog.

Over the last forty years, trainers such as Ian Dunbar, Carole Lea Benjamin, John Rogerson and

Terry Ryan have shown us that using motivation and rewards works better, works faster and is more productive than previous disciplinary methods that were originally developed for military dogs.

Even when you think you're not training your dog, you often are. Good timing is important; actually, it's vital. Give rewards such as toys, food or praise as soon as you see that your dog is thinking about doing the right thing. That may sound abstract, but it's really quite simple. When I crouch down to say hello to Lola, as soon as she gets up to move towards me I'm already rewarding her with words of praise. The reverse also applies. If I visit and she's in her playpen and whines to get out, I don't go to her because I don't want her to think that whining is an effective way to train humans.

Rewards, and discipline, should be immediate, not even seconds later. If you find a puddle on the kitchen floor, forget even mentioning it to your dog – it's too late. Harsh words just mean you're angry. Dogs are amazingly intelligent, but don't expect your dog to think in the abstract the way we do. I wish they did, but dogs don't understand conditional ideas. I might say, 'If you do that again, Lola, I'll be really, really cross,' but all Lola really understands is what Gary Larson said in his ever-so-accurate cartoon about what dogs hear: 'Blah blah blah blah blah, Lola, blah blah blah blah blah.'

'I warned you about using the wrong body language.'

Indoor preparations

Training is easier and life for your pup a lot safer if you plan ahead and dog-proof your home. Think 'safe for children' and you are almost there. What you're doing is controlling your dog's environment. If you do this, it's more likely that you can anticipate her behaviour and be prepared for the consequences. Here are suggestions for what to do indoors.

1. Remove any live electric cords to prevent electric shocks.

2. Avoid dangling electric cords. They're too much fun to tug on.

3. Move all household cleaners out of harm's way. Most are potentially dangerous.

4. Think about how you store your kitchen waste. A pedal bin is less attractive to a dog than a hanging plastic bag.

5. Don't give an old shoe or slipper to your dog to chew on. A pup can't differentiate your old shoes from your new Jimmy Choos.

6. Check out where your chewable surfaces are. Wooden kitchen table legs are ideal. Don't let your pup chew on them.

7. Temporarily remove any throw rugs and small carpets. They're too chewably attractive and difficult to clean when soiled by your as-yet-untrained puppy.

'It's your bedtime, Henry. Don't make
me have to spank you!'

Outdoor preparations

If you have a garden, yard, patio or balcony, think dog thoughts while you investigate it. Check the perimeter fence or rail to make sure it's dog-proof in two different ways: secure enough to prevent puppy escape now, and strong enough to withstand the actions of your dog when she's mature. A three-foot fence is fine for many small dogs, but you'll need a six-foot fence for agile large breeds. Make sure your fence is well-secured, especially if you have a natural digger such as a terrier.

Examine any gates to ensure they lock shut and don't have gaps underneath that a puppy or small dog can crawl through. The safest gates spring shut automatically after opening. Once more, think 'child' when you look at security. If you have a swimming pool, ensure that the fence around the pool area is puppy- as well as child-proof. If you use a pool cover, make sure it's absolutely dog-proof. Store all garden chemicals and equipment in a secure area your dog can't wander into, break into or chew into. Garbage bins are fun to knock over. Keep them in a latched box.

If your dog is to have outdoor access, examine your garden for potentially poisonous trees, shrubs and flowers; ensure your dog can't access dangerous areas. Plan where you want to place an outdoor water bowl and make sure there's a shaded area for hot weather. Prevent access to the barbecue area when cooking food. If you have a fish pond, temporarily cover it with mesh to prevent access.

If you treasure your garden, then from the first day restrict your dog to an area where she can't cause damage. This may mean an 'invisible fence': an underground wire that sends a mild shock to your dog's collar when the perimeter wire is approached. Avoid placing potted plants and plant containers where they can be knocked over. Fence off the vegetable garden and compost pile.

Prevent burnt patches on the grass by installing a sandpit toileting area for your dog, and train your dog to urinate in that specified area. If your new adult dog already urinates on the lawn, the best you can do is keep a water container handy to keep her urine dilute.

Forget about democracy

There's a great difference between training children and training dogs. As our children grow, we reason with them; they come to understand what is fair and unfair. They understand that conditions may apply. Three strikes and you are out is a situation kids learn to live with, but dogs never do.

Your dog does not have the ability to learn through abstractions. I wish she did, but she will never develop democratic ideals. Yes, some dogs have the most amazing generosity of spirit, but that's within an individual's personality, not an inherent characteristic of dogs. Dogs are naturally possessive, naturally territorial and sophisticated observers of hierarchies. They are natural opportunists and will take advantage when they can.

In your relationship with your dog, forget about consensus and democracy. Don't be a boss, but instead, be a natural leader. Dogs respond to confident leaders. Make sure your family eats before you feed your dog. Handle her routinely. Groom her every day. Go through doors first. All of these behaviours are, to a dog, obvious signs of leadership. Above all, be consistent. Never underestimate your dog's ability to see your inconsistencies and to work on them.

If you have a shy pup or dog, take extra care. They need special attention. Some breeds – German shepherds and working collies immediately come to mind – are more likely to be inherently shy than others: for example, Labradors or Jack Russell terriers. Shy breeds or individuals benefit just as much from socializing as do gregarious ones, but the introductions to the sights, smells and sounds of life need to be monitored more closely. Don't overprotect a shy dog. Protecting her from visiting children will only increase her apprehension when visitors arrive. Ask kids to be less noisy. Tell them to avoid eye

'Wait till Daddy gets home and you'll get a *real* telling off!'

contact with your puppy and give them food or toy treats to leave in a trail and eventually to give to your pup.

Do the same outdoors. Control your natural inclination to comfort when your pup is frightened by a noise or movement. If you pick her up and mutter soothing words, you're teaching her that she gets a reward when she shows signs of fear.

If you have a shy pup, it's always useful to mention this to your veterinarian, who may recommend you get a little professional help to ensure that shyness doesn't develop into lifelong fearful behaviour.

Dogs respond to consistency

Dogs thrive on consistency. As they get older, the need for consistency becomes even greater, which is the reason why older dogs are less inclined to accept change than younger ones. Dogs need and want to know the rules: what's allowed and what's not. Inconsistency is very confusing. The time for food, the time for exercise, the importance of possessions, the need to bark ('I did it before so I'll do it again') becomes a thoughtless mantra for most dogs because it reinforces their natural need for order and constancy.

Your dog wants you to be consistent in your relations with her. This is most important when giving rewards or meting out verbal discipline. Rewards are obviously positive, but when using discipline never leave your dog on a negative note. Even after a reprimand, let yourself cool down, then do something positive. Respect and friendship are the keys to a future happy relationship.

Dogs enjoy rewards

When selecting rewards, a tasty treat is just about the most potent reward you can give most dogs, especially if it's pungently smelly, like crispy, hard bits of microwaved liver. Dogs don't need 'brain-food' rewards; just about anything is fine as long as it tastes good. With many dogs, just of piece of kibble is a sufficient reward; it's almost a symbolic gesture. Keep food rewards with you whenever you go anywhere with your dog. I find that yeast-based vitamin and mineral tablets are excellent. They smell sufficiently disgusting for dogs to love them while not too disgusting to keep in your pocket or purse.

Toys are almost as powerful rewards as food, especially chewable or squeaky toys. Use toys as rewards for dogs that are not piggy by nature. As a breed, German shepherds respond well to toys as rewards. Be careful with toys, however. They belong to you, not your dog, and are only given to your dog as rewards. An ideal toy is one small enough for you to hide in your pocket, but big enough not to cause a danger from choking.

Sometimes you have to build up interest if you want to use a toy. If this is the case, do silly things with it. Produce it from your pocket, sniff it and put it back. Talk to it. Wave it at your dog then put it on a shelf. Your aim is to trigger your dog's interest and desire to possess it.

A soothing lick from mother was comforting to your pup. So, too, is a gentle hand stroke on the body from you. Use contact comfort as an important reward when your dog responds well. Associate touch with food rewards and words of praise. It's always good to train a dog to be touched while she's eating. Later I'll explain how training your dog to let you take her food away while she eats reduces the risks of her becoming possessive and guarding it from people or other animals.

At the same time as you give a potent reward such as food, a toy or touch, give a verbal reward. Your dog soon learns that just the words 'Good girl,' or 'Good boy' are satisfying on their own. In your relationship with your dog, start with a potent reward and graduate to using less powerful secondary rewards: words alone. Be precise with the words you use when speaking to your dog. She understands black and white, not shades of grey. Think 'yes' or 'no' – never 'maybe' – when speaking, or for that matter interacting in any way with your dog.

If your dog becomes too excited by food or a toy as a reward, ignore her and go away. Repeat what you were trying to do when she's calmer, using a less potent reward such as words alone. If she's not interested in responding to any of your rewards, schedule activities just before feeding time, when she's most alert. Use a little hand-held attention-getting noise-maker.

Dogs understand discipline

There will be occasions when discipline is needed. Use it as wisely as you use rewards. The word 'No!' is a powerful word – strong medicine. Use it only when you see your dog doing something wrong. Don't shriek it, mumble it, whine it or use it so frequently that your dog disregards it. Growl it, deeply and sharply, whenever you use it.

Dogs don't use discipline to get even (although there will be times when your dog pushes you so far all you'll want to do is get even). Dogs use discipline to assert authority, and that's how you should use it. Use a variety of different forms of discipline to help your dog learn what's acceptable and what's not.

I haven't said to teach your dog right from wrong because that's not what you're teaching. In your dog's mind, it's right to howl when separated from her family. It's right to chew on hard objects. It's right to guard her own food. What she learns from you is not right or wrong but acceptable and unacceptable. Interchange forms of discipline so that she always has the potential to be surprised by what you do.

As I've said, don't overuse the word 'No' when giving verbal discipline. 'Bad dog!' said crisply is a good phrase. Personally, I like 'Arghhh!' It is a bit like what a pup's mother used to say to her miscreant pup. One of my nurses has brought her pug Alice to work each day since Alice was a pup. All of us giggled ourselves silly as we heard 'Arghhh!' coming from all parts of the clinic. The end result, however, was great. All Hilary has to do now is lift her right lip as if she's going to 'Arghhh!' and Alice stops what she's not supposed to be doing and returns to her bed.

Dogs know the difference between being looked at and being given the eyeball. Dominant dogs stare down others. You can use the same method, especially from the advantage of your height. Standing over your dog, saying 'Bad dog!' then maintaining your stare is an excellent form of discipline. Eventually, just the look is enough.

Dogs are intensely social. They don't like being separated from family activity. Use symbolic isolation as another potent form of discipline. By symbolic, I mean for its shock value, not as a form of retribution. If, for example, your pup bites you too hard during play, emit your well-practised high-pitched shriek, get up, leave the room and shut the door. Wait half a minute then go back in, disregard your dog for another minute, then do what you want. If too many other people are in the room, take your dog to an empty room (the bathroom, for example) shut the door, count to thirty, then let her out, disregarding her for another minute or so.

There are times when harsh words, the evil eye or isolation aren't enough. Something more dramatic is needed to get your dog to pay attention or to stop what she's doing. This is where 'theatrics' – water pistols, noise-makers, even a symbolic shake by the scruff of the neck – are effective. Scruff shakes are similar to what mother does when she's annoyed by puppy mayhem, but use this form of discipline sparingly and wisely. You don't want your dog to become shy of your touch, nor do you want to provoke an aggressive response. The key to success with all these methods is that it should be unexpected. 'Whahappend!?' is what you want your dog to think.

Getting good results

Whatever the rewards or discipline, good results depend on good timing. Give the reward – food, toys, touch or praise – as soon as your dog tries to do the right thing. Rewards given too late, even three seconds after the event, cause confusion, especially in young pups. Good timing is a skill that some people naturally have and an aptitude that others have to learn. Fortunately, older dogs learn to understand that some people can sometimes be a bit clumsy with timing. Stay alert. Concentrate. Poor timing is confusing to pups in particular and gets your relationship off to a poor start.

Whatever happens, no matter how much your dog amuses or irritates you, try to remember that you're both her leader and her friend. Good relations and responsiveness from your dog depend upon her seeing you as the individual who makes decisions and issues commands. If she thinks she's your equal, you lose respect. If you lose respect, she'll not respond to you as leader.

At the same time, you want her to be relaxed, not tense. If you're her friend, she'll want to please you because she so enjoys your praise when she does something right. That, in a nutshell is the attractiveness of dogs: their open, giving desire to please. Don't turn it into fear through punishment, or disdain through inconsistency. A wonderful relationship will develop, but it depends upon you using calm logic and a positive attitude and being consistent. Time devoted to good training pays dividends for years to come.

'I *am* house-trained, but I didn't
know they meant other people's houses…'

chapter five
HOW TO HOUSE-TRAIN YOUR DOG

Canine sanitary habits can make or break your relationship with your dog. If house training goes well, easy obedience training almost inevitably follows. Dogs are instinctively clean animals, unwilling to soil their own nests. It's up to us to take advantage of this fact and teach them that the entire home is 'the nest'.

Fortunately, the instinct not to soil the nest is already there in young pups. House-training takes advantage of that instinct by restricting a dog to her 'nest' and taking her to the location where you want her to toilet. After 'success', your dog is rewarded by being given access to other parts of the home. House-training is simple, but it depends upon your vigilance.

Basic puppy house-training

It's easiest to house-train a dog if you have immediate access to a yard or garden. Flat-dwellers and disabled people have a few more logistics problems, but wherever you live, and whoever you are, aim for the following.

- Select a toileting area away from activity and distractions.

- In the garden, yard or public place, choose an area that is easy to clean.

- Have scoops (such as a plastic bag) always available. Clean up immediately after your dog defecates. Scooping is simpler from a hard surface than from grass.

A pup is pre-programmed for house-training. She doesn't want to soil her nest and naturally wants to relieve herself after eating, after play or exercise, after any excitement such as a greeting, and after waking up. As a very young puppy, she'll need an opportunity to empty her bladder every hour. She will also need a toilet time last thing at night. Watch your pup's body language for these clues:

- Sniffing the floor

- Circling

- Running with the nose to the floor

- Getting ready to squat

When you see any of these activities, interrupt her and take her outside. If you can, avoid picking her up. You want her to learn that she should walk to the back door when she needs to relieve herself.

Dogs (and cats for that matter) are inherently clean animals, which is a powerful reason why we chose them as our favourite house pets. As I've mentioned, a dog instinctively feels comfortable in the security of its own den and doesn't want to mess in it. A dog crate is a natural den. It may look like a jail to us, but it isn't to a dog, unless we use it wrongly.

Dogs like crates – the same as dogs like going under kitchen tables, or behind sofas or under beds.

Your dog's crate should be comfortable and contain activities for her amusement, but it should not be so large that she can leave her bedding and mess in another part of it. Plan ahead when getting a crate so that it's useful for your dog when she's adult size. Use a large cardboard carton to block off a section of the crate so that it's not too large an area for her as a puppy.

Crate-training speeds up house-training enormously because a dog is either in her crate, out of her crate toileting where you want her to toilet, or discovering the rest of the world because she's just emptied both tanks. A crate gives you time to concentrate on other matters rather than on your pup for twenty-four hours each day.

Garden or yard training

This is the ideal. At the times I've mentioned, take your pup outdoors and go out with her. You want her to be relaxed. If she's out and you're in, she may concentrate on wanting to get back to you rather than relieving herself. She sees you standing inside the door and wants to be with you. She gets excited trying to get in. You conclude that she's not going to relieve herself because she's not concentrating so you let her in. Within a few minutes, she's messed inside. The result is a mess for you to clean up and a pup that attended the wrong school.

Wear the right clothes, take an umbrella if necessary, but be prepared to be outside for four or five minutes while she sniffs and wanders. Wait patiently. Don't play games; be still and silent. Use word cues you're happy to have heard in public, when toilet training your dog. With time, she'll associate hearing these words with the need to go. 'Hurry up' is a practical word cue.

As she starts to pee or poo, say the word or words you've chosen to be associated with her relieving herself. Later, hearing these words will stimulate her to relieve herself. After she's finished give her sufficient praise to make her tail wag. If the weather permits, stay out a little longer. Play a game. Most dogs love the opportunity to be outdoors. If, after five minutes, she hasn't relieved herself, return indoors but keep an eagle eye on her activity so you're prepared for a quick return.

When you see your dog starting to relieve herself in the house, get her attention by shouting – not to frighten or punish her, but rather to get her mind on you. If you frighten her, or if she thinks you're angry, unwittingly you'll teach her to be more selective with her toileting. She'll learn to sneak away to relieve herself, making it harder for you to train her.

As soon as you have her attention, call her name then briskly walk to your back door. You want to encourage her willingly to follow you outside where, after the excitement of watching you has subsided, she'll complete what she started earlier. When you return to the house, keep her in another room while you clean up her mess.

Don't punish your dog for what she's done earlier; she won't get it. What she'll think is that you're angry with her and she'll respond by acting submissively. She does this to appease you: to extinguish the flame of your anger. We make the mistake of thinking that her signs of appeasement are signs of guilt; they're not. I cannot emphasize this enough. Punishing after the fact is always counterproductive. You're only teaching her that you're unpredictable. Punishment when you return to a mess in the house is interpreted as punishment when you return.

Apartment training

Housetraining without access to a garden or yard is a bit more complicated and more time-consuming on your part, but it follows the same principles as yard or garden training. First, choose the area near your flat where it's safe and acceptable for your dog to toilet. The closer the better, but of course, this isn't always possible. This makes the hourly visit to the great outdoors even more important than for garden training. You've got to be extra-vigilant. If this isn't

'Bad dog!'

'That's not one of mine.'

practical then indoor paper-training to newspaper, a litter tray or commercially produced disposable pet pads becomes the pragmatic second choice.

Paper-training is, realistically, a practical way to train apartment pups, but remember: if you use this method, you prolong the training period. You're training your pup to mess on paper, then later when she has control of her bladder and bowels, you retrain her not to mess on paper but rather to mess outdoors.

If not using a crate, the easiest way to paper-train is to restrict your pup to one room or one area of a room where the floor has been covered in plastic sheeting, on top of which you lay lots of newspaper. In these circumstances, your pup can only relieve herself on the newspaper. You'll see over a few days that she prefers several specific spots.

When removing soiled newspaper, save small bits to place in the areas where you want your dog to urinate. It takes less than a week for a pup to be trained to eliminate in these areas. Day by day, you reduce the paper-covered areas until only a few are needed. At the same time, take your dog out as frequently as possible so that she learns to use her outdoor toilet as well. Just as with any other form of house-training, only let your pup investigate other parts of your home after she's pooped and peed on her litter tray, piddle pad or newspaper. The frequency of her need to empty her bladder and bowels decreases as your pup matures.

The sensitivity of a dog's nose is simply beyond our comprehension. Routine cleaning and disinfecting may mask odours for us, but it won't get rid of the residual odours left by messing. These natural smells draw your dog back to the site, so it's vitally important to break down odour molecules. Your vet can supply you with enzyme-containing odour-eliminators. In my experience, these work well. As an alternative, mix biological (enzyme-containing) washing powder with hot water and liberally soak the area. Alcohol will also break down odours.

Avoid any cleanser with ammonia. Ammonia is a natural body by-product; it will attract rather than repel a dog. If carpet is soiled, the underlay and even the floor beneath should be treated with any odour-eliminating product. White vinegar and water is good for removing stains from carpets.

It's fascinating how fast something so young can learn to be house-trained, but remember: she's a puppy at heart until well after she reaches physical maturity at say, one year of age. Expect lapses in these circumstances:

•Sexual maturity

•Sudden household activity, such as a party

•Changes in who is her primary 'leader'

•Emotional turmoil in the family

•The arrival of another pet

House-training adult dogs

All the principles of toilet training apply equally to older dogs. The important difference is that some older dogs have to 'unlearn' some toileting habits before learning new ones. Crate training is ideal, although an older dog not used to a crate will need to be conditioned to the idea of using it.

In this instance, I'd suggest a sturdy plastic crate that comes apart in the middle, leaving the bottom much like a typical dog's bed. Get the older dog used to this bed, then after several days, reassemble the crate, keep the door open and toss a little food or favourite toys in. Serve meals in it if you like, but don't close the door. Get your dog used to spending time in it with the door open. This works fastest when the crate is in your own bedroom at night.

Adult dogs can control their bowels and bladder far longer than pups, so they can be crated for longer periods of time. When she's in a crate, make sure your dog has amusements to keep her occupied: for example, a chew toy with soft cheese spread in the hollow middle. Take her out as you would a pup, at least four times a day, but eliminate the hourly yard visits and always give your 'Hurry up' or 'Do it' command as she does it, followed by praise.

If you're not using a crate, your older dog should be tethered to you and not allowed to roam the house freely until after she has relieved herself outdoors. If she starts to pee or poop, correct her with a sharp 'No!' then immediately take her outside. Of course praise her with your most impressive 'Good girl' when she performs where you want her to.

The key to success is to limit the chances of her messing where you don't want her to mess. Be consistent. Accidents will happen, but keep your cool. If accidents are happening frequently, it's your fault because you're not keeping close enough tabs on her. Be consistent and patient. Any adult dog can learn the essence of house-training within two weeks. If training is taking you longer, contact your vet to ensure there are no medical problems (such as incontinence due to muscle weakness) and for advice on the professional dog trainers in your locality.

Anticipate problems

Dogs have great biological clocks that work best when you create daily routines. Feeding times are important. What goes in at a certain time comes out at a certain time. This is why the late-evening meal is the first to be dropped as a puppy matures. Use this love of routine to your advantage by associating toileting with a really powerful reward: going for a stimulating walk.

'I *tried* telling you!'

Try to ensure that your timetable lets you take your dog into the garden or backyard for her to relieve herself, back in if she doesn't, back out for a second try and only after success do you take her for a walk. If you're gutter-training her, follow the same routine: out to the gutter, a maximum five minute hang around, then back inside and out again for another try. Only after successful toileting in the gutter do you wind her up with praise and an active, exciting walk.

Some dogs become house-trained during the day but mess at night. If your dog is over five months old and behaving like this, she's probably developed a habit of messing at night. It's very unlikely that physiologically she needs to relieve herself. In these circumstances, she should sleep in your bedroom in a crate. When she needs to relieve herself, she'll whine. Just get up and take her outside. Next night, when she whines again, lie there in bed for a few moments then take her out. No fuss: out and in. The next night, wait ten minutes. Over a two-week period you'll train her body to wait until morning.

When training is complete she returns to wherever you want her to sleep.

Dogs urinate to empty full bladders, but they also urinate when they're frightened. Even more frequently, females in particular urinate as a sign of submission. Don't mistake this for a lapse in house-training. Submissively urinating is the natural way a low-ranking dog appeases a high-ranking one. This is why urinating when excited is more a puppy than an adult problem; most pups look upon us big humans as naturally high-rankers.

If your pup piddles when she sees you, don't reprimand her or show anger. Don't even touch her. These are the actions of high-rankers. Instead, ignore her, walk away, either to an area where there's newspaper on plastic sheeting, or out the back door where she can relieve herself. Most pups outgrow submissive urinating as they mature and build confidence. Curiously, these pups are the easiest to obedience-train because they concentrate so intently on you, but it's absolutely imperative to avoid scolding or anger during training. If your dog urinates submissively, keep plastic sheeting and an absorbent towel inside the front door so you're prepared for mishaps during the time necessary to bolster your dog's self-confidence.

Finally, training more than one dog at a time is extremely difficult. A crate becomes almost imperative for easy training of two or more pups at the same time. As with all training, it's important that only one dog at a time hears appropriate word signals.

'I've discovered that whining usually
gets their attention...'

'OFF!'

chapter six
HOW TO CARRY OUT BASIC TRAINING

Teaching good manners – to come, stay, sit or lie down – is surprisingly easy. Most dogs willingly carry out these activities because they want to please their leaders and because it's in their interest to do so. When your dog respects you as a leader and when she knows her name, she's ready for simple obedience training. This is easiest with puppies because they naturally look up to you as a strong leader. Older dogs take longer to accept a new person as their leader, but through your confident and consistent behaviour a dog learns to respect you. Train your dog when both her mind and yours are alert. Remember, use body language as well as words and combine these with rewards. Good timing is vital. Finally, don't ask your dog to do something you can't ensure she'll do.

The essentials of basic training

Plan ahead. Start as you mean to continue. Use specific words combined with specific hand or body signals as commands. Write them down. Make sure everyone in the family uses the same words and signals.

Train when both you and your dog are mentally alert. An ideal time to train is just before feeding time. With pups, that means you have three or four ready-prepared training opportunities each day. As your pup matures and the number of meals diminishes, train her shortly after she wakes up and after she's emptied her bladder and bowels. At first, always combine food rewards with praise. Eventually, only give the most powerful reward, food, intermittently. Giving rewards intermittently, rather than constantly is the most effective way to reinforce learning.

Avoid distractions. Inside your own home is the easiest place to begin training. This applies to simple obedience such as come-sit-stay-down but also to leash training or 'walking-to-heel' training:

'Come, go, fetch, sit, boil me an
egg... Make up your mind!'

walking beside you. A hallway is an almost ideal place to begin training because it's such a boring place to be. Once your dog reliably responds in that location, move on to a more distracting environment – the back garden, for example. When your dog reliably responds to training in these locations, advance to more complicated surroundings: the street or a park. Train by increments. Avoid leaps from one level to a much higher one.

Keep lessons short. A minute or two is perfect for a pup; five minutes is too long. Older dogs have greater powers of concentration, but even those with the best mental stamina can't concentrate on training for more than about fifteen minutes at a time.

Keep lessons enjoyable. If she's not enjoying herself, forget about training. The opposite applies, too. If she's over-the-top with energy, let her use up some of that energy first. Once that's out of her system, she'll concentrate more on what you're doing with her.

Don't get flustered. Avoid repeatedly shouting a command – it only confuses your dog. If training isn't going well, stop. Think about what you're doing. The problem is with *you*, not with your dog.

Virtually all dogs have the capacity to learn basic obedience in a short period of time – within days for some and a maximum of a few weeks for dogs that need reprogramming. Don't be bashful about asking for help. Front-office staff at veterinary clinics are probably your best bet for sound advice.

Finally, always finish on a positive note. These short episodes each day should be fun for both of you. Play with your pup, but don't save the most powerful reward for the end of the session. If you do, unwittingly you're training your dog to want the session to end so she can get hold of the potent reward.

Teaching the command 'come'

This is the easiest command for a dog to learn. Mealtime provides an ideal teaching opportunity.

•Crouch down a short distance away from your dog, show her the food bowl, say her name and as she begins to move towards her meal give the command 'Come'.

•As she approaches, say 'Good girl!' with enthusiasm.

•Give her the meal.

Between meals, carry out the same exercise a few times daily, using a food tidbit as the reward. Graduate to standing upright while getting her attention by calling her name, then saying 'Come' as she starts to approach. Stroke her as an alternative reward. Within a few days she'll come to you willingly when she hears her name and the word 'Come'.

Older, strong-willed or shy dogs may not come so willingly. To ensure that your dog always complies with your instructions, use a thin 'house line' (a very long, thin leash.) to ensure you can always get your dog's attention. Don't use the line like a fishing line to reel in your dog; she'll put up automatic resistance. Give a quick jerk on the line to get your dog's attention, then draw her to you with your reward.

It's easy to make unintentional mistakes during basic training. Never say 'Come' unless you're sure your dog will obey; never use it to call your dog from something exciting to something less interesting. And never use it to call your dog to discipline her.

'Come, Spot!'

Teaching the command 'sit'

Dogs learn 'Sit' as quickly as they learn the command 'Come'. Concentrate on your dog's head. Control her head, and her body will do what you want it to do.

•Stand facing your dog with her food bowl or a food treat in your hand and command her to 'Come'.

•When she reaches you, hold her food or treat over her head. Make sure she has eye contact with her reward. As her head follows the food above her, her rump will naturally go down. When she bends her hind legs, give the command 'Sit'.

•As she assumes a sitting position, say 'Good girl' and give the food immediately.

Once she's obediently sitting as she faces you, graduate to standing beside her while giving the command 'Sit'. At first, always give food rewards but eventually give them intermittently. Ultimately words of praise alone should be sufficient.

Most dogs naturally assume a sitting position to keep an eye on something above them; some don't. If your dog doesn't sit for a food reward, hold her collar in one hand and use your other hand to tuck her hindquarters into a sitting position. Give the command 'Sit' as you do this and instantly reward her with a food treat and a verbal 'Good girl'. Avoid over-excitement. If meals are too exciting, your dog can't concentrate on commands. Train her on a fuller stomach, using less stimulating but still interesting rewards. Once more, never give a command without ensuring your dog complies. If you do, you're actively training your dog to disregard that command.

'I thought you said "Sit".'

Teaching the command 'stay'

The third command in the sequence is 'Stay' or 'Wait'. This is vital for a dog's future safety and is simply a prolonged variation of 'Sit'. After you've trained your dog to 'Sit' for verbal praise, graduate to 'Stay', reinforcing the command with your chosen hand signal.

- Ensure your dog's head is up, looking at your face (but she shouldn't be looking up vertically.)

- After she sits, show her the palm of your hand while you command 'Stay'.

- Initially keep the duration of the 'Sit-Stay' short, then calmly give a small food reward.

- Gradually increase the duration of the 'Stay', also graduating to the command word alone without the food treat.

- Repeat the exercise for a week, gradually backing away until you're giving the command at a distance. Complete 'Stay' by introducing a release word, such as 'Finished'. Reward her.

Try training with your dog sitting at the base of a wall; that keeps her from sliding backwards. If your dog does not respond properly or does something wrong, avoid the word 'No'. Save that for more serious misdemeanours.

Introduce a neutral word when she doesn't get it right – I like 'Wrong'. If, for example she rolls on her back, say 'Wrong', stand up and induce her back into a 'Sit' position. Avoid an abundance of praise after releasing your dog from 'Stay'. Too much praise on your part winds her up and teaches her to jump around and be exuberant at the end of a training session. Keep your praise muted.

Never try 'Stay' training in situations where your dog finds it difficult to concentrate on what you're doing. If she's worried about the presence of other dogs or more interested in investigating other activities, her mind is elsewhere. During each short training session you want her rapt attention.

Teaching the command 'lie down'

'Lie down' is a natural variation of 'Sit' and 'Stay' but requires a little more work on your part and understanding by your dog. All commands so far have anticipated a willing response from your dog. Now, you're commanding her to do something natural but at the same time, a little unusual.

- With your pup in a 'Sit' position, kneel to her right, hold her collar with your left hand and hold a food treat in your right.

- Put the food treat in front of your pup's nose, then, using a sweeping action, move your treat-holding hand forward and downward in an arc. As your pup lies down to keep in contact with the now ground-level food treat, give the command 'Down'. Keep the treat clenched in your hand so she can't grab it.

- Continue moving the food along the floor until she is in a complete down position. Praise her with 'Good girl' and give her the treat.

•Once she understands 'Down', prolong it with 'Stay', rewarding her good response initially with both food and praise, then food intermittently with praise, and finally with verbal praise alone.

•Release her from her 'Down-Stay' with the release word 'Finished'.

If your pup creeps forward on her haunches, kneel beside her; while she's sitting, put the palms of your hands under her forelegs, lift gently into a begging position then lower into a lying position. Instantly reward her with praise and treats. If she refuses to stay down, use both hands to apply gentle pressure to her withers: the area above her shoulders. Reward her for lying down, then release her with the word 'Finished'.

You're teaching your dog a new language, so be patient and reasonable. Don't bore your dog with periods of training that are too frequent or too long. Remember, a few minutes two or three times a day is just about right for most dogs (mature dogs can cope with fifteen minute sessions twice a day).

Teaching walking to heel

The most common behaviour question I'm asked at the veterinary clinic is, 'How can I stop my dog pulling on her leash?' It's simple, but depends on your dog already understanding basic obedience. She must understand 'Sit' because this is always the take-off point for walking to heel.

Traditionally, dogs are trained to walk by your left side. The tradition evolved out of gun-dog training: the dog walks to the left while the handler carries his shotgun and shoots from the right. The dog is always at the handler's heel – which of course is why training is called 'heel training'. If you plan to participate in any type of dog-training classes in future, it's better to begin as they will have you continue. Otherwise, it doesn't matter which side your dog is on.

Start practice training in your home, but first always let your dog play vigorously to burn up excess energy. Get her used to the feeling of the leash by attaching it to her collar and using it when training her to 'Come' to you. Train in a hallway where there are no distractions before progressing to the garden. Always keep first sessions short, beginning with a few seconds and a few feet forward. Repeat this twice a day, increasing both time and distance. It doesn't matter whether you start heel training on or off the leash. It's not an issue of right or wrong, but rather what feels best for you and your dog. Use food treats and praise in the following sequence.

Walking off the leash
•Position your pup in a 'Sit' to your left (if that's the side you've chosen) and, holding her collar with your left hand, say her name to get her attention. Let her scent the food treat in your clenched fist.

   •As you step forward with your left foot and she follows the scent of the treat, give the command 'Heel' (or 'Walk', if you prefer).

   •After only a few steps give the command 'Wait', get down to her level (to prevent jumping up) and give her the food reward. If it's necessary, use your free left arm, extended under her belly to prevent her from moving forward out of the 'Wait' position. Repeat the exercise but don't overdo it. With each lesson extend the distance you move in a straight line.

When your pup responds well to 'walk' and 'wait' in a straight line, introduce swings to the left and right.

•Walk forward, with your pup, at your left, responding. Keeping your right hand with the food treat low in front of your pup's nose, give the command 'Heel' as you turn to the right.

•Your pup speeds up because she has farther to go when turning right. After a few steps in the new direction, give the command 'Wait', stop and reward good behaviour with the food treat and kind words.

•Left turns are at first more awkward for both of you. With your pup walking forward at your left, give the command 'Steady' as you move your right hand holding the food treat in front of you and to the left.

•Your pup slows down (and soon learns that 'Steady' means 'Slow down') as her nose leads the rest of her body to the left. You may need to guide a left turn with your hand on her collar. Once she's turned left and taken a few steps, give the command 'Wait', stop and reward her good behaviour with the food treat and kind words.

If your puppy jumps up to get at the treat, you're holding it too high. Move your hand lower and at the same time use your free left hand on your dog's collar to prevent jumping. If your pup is an obsessive foodie, try training for a few minutes after meals.

If your pup loses concentration, you've probably chosen the wrong time or place for training. Try again when she's better prepared. If, during training, she's distracted from what you're teaching her, use your left hand on her collar to bring her back to the correct 'Heel' position, get her attention with the food treat and continue. If a distraction is overwhelming, command her to do something you know she'll do (a 'Sit') reward her with verbal praise and continue later when the distraction isn't there.

Walking on the leash
When a puppy willingly follows you off-leash, it's easy to graduate to walking-to-heel training on a leash. Use a leash with a collar clasp of appropriate weight for your dog. If you haven't introduced the leash before, let your pup look at it and smell it.

•Attach the leash to your puppy's well-fitted, comfortable collar. With the pup to your left, hold the end of the leash and the food treat in your right hand; your left hand holds the slack in the leash. Avoid tension on the leash. Command your pup to 'Sit'.

•Start walking forward (with your left foot) and as your puppy gets up to move, give the command 'Heel'. Let her feel only the slightest tension on the leash. If she surges forward, slide your hand down the leash, give a slight jerk and the command 'Steady'.

•After a few steps give the command 'Wait', get down to her level (to prevent jumping up) and give her the food reward. Verbally reward her, then try the procedure again covering the same sequence of events.

•Once she's walking to heel on her leash in a straight line, graduate to turns. Guide her to the right as I've described above, with the food in your left hand, and as she turns in that direction, give the command 'Heel'. Teach left turns by increasing your speed at first, rather than having your puppy decrease hers. With the leash in your right hand, slide your left hand down the slack to your puppy's collar. Guide her nose to the left with the treat in your right hand.

•When she has learned to turn left at her regular speed, repeat the manoeuvre with you walking at your regular speed and her slowing down. As she slows down, give the command 'Steady' (or 'Slow', if your prefer).

Don't expect your dog to be an angel. If she tries to climb her leash, say 'No!', move away, give the command 'Sit' and go back to the beginning of the exercise. If she thinks it's more fun to chew the leash than walk attached to it, invest in an unpleasant-tasting but safe chew deterrent such as bitter-apple spray. Spray the parts of the leash likely to be chewed.

Some pups collapse because they're overly submissive. Others do it because it's a giggle. Submissive pups need active encouragement to stand on all fours. Be gentle and patient. Use a favourite squeaky toy as encouragement and plenty of praise to build confidence. Gigglers need to be reminded there's a time for play and a time for concentration. If your puppy collapses in fits of fun when you put her leash on, get her into a 'Sit', and get her full concentration before proceeding with leash training.

Graduate to real-world walking exercises after you've trained your dog to walk to heel in the quiet of your home and garden. When your dog hears the word 'Heel', it learns that it means 'Walk close and pay constant attention to me'. Even if you're a steady walker, vary the speed of your walk to give your dog the stimulation of the unexpected and of variety. If your dog gets distracted – and she will – then get excited, get enthusiastic or get theatrical, but get her attention back to you.

A few more basic commands

'LEAVE IT' There are some objects you'll want your dog to leave alone, for her safety as well as for other reasons. All dogs should understand the command 'Leave it' or 'Leave'. Also, male dogs always sniff first before urine-marking. The 'Leave it' command works as well to stop leg-lifting where you don't want legs lifted as it does to prevent scavenging.

•Put your dog in a 'Sit-stay', and get down on your haunches. Hold a food treat in one hand while making a fist (thumb and forefinger up) with the other. As she reaches for the treat, pop her gently under the jaw with enough pressure to close her jaws but not so much that it hurts. As you do so, say 'Leave it'.

'Daisy, are you listening to me?'

•Offer the treat again and repeat the exercise. Continue to do so until she hesitates or turns away. When she does so, verbally praise her but do not give the food reward. Most dogs learn 'Leave it' very quickly.

'OFF' This is a vital command if you don't want your dog on the furniture.

•If your dog gets on the sofa, couch or bed without your permission, take her by the collar, say 'Off!', then lead her down to the floor then praise her.

•If your dog is a persistent offender or if there's even a hint of aggression from her, leave her leash (or a house line) attached to her collar while she's indoors. When you see her on something she shouldn't be on, give a slight jerk on the leash, aiming in the downward direction you want her to go in. When her feet hit the ground, command her to 'Sit', then praise her.

'GO TO BED' There will be times when you want your dog to 'disappear'. This command is really just an extension of 'Down-stay'.

• While standing near your dog's bed, call her by name.

• When she comes to you, say 'Go to bed' as you lead her to it. At the bed, issue the command 'Down-stay'.

This command takes a little practice and you must be absolutely consistent, but it's a great command to use when you're busy or when you have guests who aren't quite the dog-lovers you and your family are.

'Go to bed – hey… it's working!'

chapter seven
WHY DOGS BECOME DELINQUENTS

Hunger, sex, aggression, territory-marking… all of these are normal behaviours shared by all animals. Yet some of us are surprised when our dogs scavenge or mount visitors legs or urinate on curtains or bark and bite. We want our dogs to be ideal canine citizens. It's possible to get close to that ideal, but it involves understanding – on our part – about why dogs behave the way they do and how what we do influences their behaviour. Of all the problems dogs can develop, the most serious – for both of us – is aggression.

I know it sounds pie-in-the-sky, but a well-raised dog doesn't take up a life of crime. We're a great influence on a dog's behaviour. Cambridge University scientists made a fascinating observation when they studied aggression in cocker spaniels. They were studying aggression in this breed because red or blond cockers are more likely to show sudden dominance aggression than are other cockers with two or more coat colours.

The scientists had owners fill in self-assessment questionnaires about their own personalities and found a direct relationship between dominance-aggression problems in cockers and 'pushover' personalities in cocker owners. Their findings indicate that he more of a pushover you are, the more likely it is that your dog will develop its potential to become dominantly aggressive.

It may be difficult to alter your personality, but you can certainly make sure your dog learns about life by having as full and as stimulating an early life as possible. This is the best way to ensure that aggression problems are unlikely to develop.

Why dogs bite and show aggression

Dogs don't bite for the heck of it. There's always a reason – although it's not always obvious to us. Our problem is that we fail to see the warning signs, or if we do, we do nothing about them. Once aggressive behaviour develops, it never disappears on its own. We have to contain it, reduce it, and then eliminate it.

Ask yourself these questions about your own dog. Does your dog:

- growl at you, other people or other animals?
- show her teeth to you or your family?
- snap when you try to take a toy or food away?
- cringe or hide behind you when visitors approach?
- bark and run to the door when delivery people arrive?
- nip at your ankles when playing exuberantly?
- chase after moving objects?
- give you a hard stare that lasts for minutes?
- make you make up excuses for her aggressive behaviour, telling friends that 'It's just a phase'?
- not worry you because she is a Yorkie, not a pit bull and her pushy behaviour is 'cute'?

If you answer 'Yes' to any one of these questions, your dog has the potential to become aggressive.

The potential for aggression is greater in some breeds, or lines within breeds, than in others, but problems only occur in homes that wittingly or unwittingly encourage the development of a dog's aggressive potential.

Early socializing to the human family, to strangers, to other animals and to a whole range of experiences dramatically reduces the likelihood that a dog will reach its 'aggression potential'. Let me use the pit bull as an example. Because of its genetic tendency towards aggression and the extreme power of its jaw muscles, a pit bull is a worrisome breed. Yet in my practice I've seen many well-mannered pit bulls, properly socialized to friends and strangers. Personally, I'd never recommend getting a breed like a pit bull. The instinct to chase and kill anything small is too great. What I am saying, however, is that early learning is the most powerful tool for reducing the risk of aggression in your dog.

There are many different types of aggression, equally shared by males and females (I'll get to those shortly), but there's no doubt what statistics show: aggression is more likely to become a problem in adolescent male dogs. You and your family are the prime targets.

The reason is the pecking order. When dogs reach sexual and emotional maturity, some of the worries of puppyhood fall away. Some dogs go for higher rank in the pack and challenge people they feel have lower rank – often children. At the same time, sex hormone induces rivalry with other male dogs. Most of the

'Are you looking at me, John?'

dog-fight injuries I treat are a result of two male dogs fighting with each other. Again, good socializing is the best way to avoid these problems, as well as hormone control, which I'll also discuss in more detail shortly.

Pups rarely bite with aggressive intent until they're about seven months old, unless they're really scared or really bold. Until that age, they cope with problems by hiding, running away or doing the 'I'm not worthy' routine. Then confidence grows. A dog uses body language to express his feelings: raising his hackles, giving an intent stare, raising his tail. If this doesn't work, a growl or teeth-baring follows. And if that fails, aggression ensues to sort out the situation.

Most breeds (the German shepherd is a classic example) have superb body language, making it easy for us to read their minds. Other breeds (the Rottweiler, say) skip several language clues and go from play to aggression very quickly. This makes it difficult to read their plans, and makes the breed more dangerous to non-doggy people.

Different types of aggression

There's a whole variety of different forms of aggression, each with its own cause and treatment. It's important to understand exactly what's going on when your dog shows aggression. Biting you because you touched her where it hurts is perfectly understandable aggression on your dog's part. On the other hand, biting you because you tried to push her off the sofa is a crime. This is serious business. Unless the cause and cure are obvious, you should not rely simply on a book to overcome an aggression problem. Get help from your veterinary clinic or local dog-training club.

Dominance aggression

This is often directed against you and your family and is the most common reason why dogs growl at or bite their owners. You might think the growl or bite was sudden, but it wasn't. You dog's been assessing your position for some time and has decided to challenge. If your dog shows signs of dominance, take the following steps.

•Avoid physical punishment. It's too provoca-
tive and may make matters worse.

•Use body posture, facial expression and the
tone of your voice to leave him in no doubt
that you're the leader of the pack.

•Attach a leash or house line to your dog's collar.
Use this to move your dog to a temporary (one
minute) isolation from the family. In this way,
you reassert your authority over a pushy dog.

•Don't hold a grudge but review your relationship with your dog to determine why he thought
he could challenge you. For example, remember
you eat first, you go first through doorways. It's
the little things that give signals to your dog.

Dominance aggression between two dogs is more
likely to occur when both are relatively equal: same
sex, age and size. Some breeds such as the
Dobermann are more prone to aggression between
equals than are others. Overcoming this problem
depends upon you determining or even deciding

which is the higher-ranking dog, then treating him or her as such. Your instinct to comfort the underdog only increases the problem. The highest rank eats first, is petted by you first and goes out the door first.

If aggression is severe and this doesn't work, get your veterinarian's help. Neutering one lowers its rank. This often cures the problem. It may seem heartless to neuter the underdog, but this is usually enough to stop dominance fighting.

Sex-related aggression

Sex-related aggression occurs year-round in males but only twice a year in females, when they're hormonally active. Maternal aggression is probably the most fearsome type of aggression that exists. Mothers don't mess about; they mean it when they say they'll do anything to protect their litter. Early socializing to a variety of people reduces the likelihood of maternal aggression when a bitch has a litter, but there's a curiosity in canines that is different to all other domestic animals. Regardless of whether she's pregnant or not, after ovulating all females go through a two-month hormonal pregnancy. During the latter part of this 'phantom pregnancy', a female may become possessive over certain items: shoes, soft toys, socks. She might hoard them under the bed or table and be possessive of them. This is a form of maternal aggression, showing itself as possessiveness. The problem can be avoided through early neutering.

Male-to-male aggression is a more common form of sex-related aggression. This is more likely to occur in dogs that as pups were allowed to play rough games without correction. To reduce the risks of this type of aggression, don't let your pup do any of the following:

- Bite other dogs hard.

- Put his paws on another dog's back

- Mount and thrust on any part of another dog.

Tolerant, older family dogs often let pups get away with these activities. If a pup gets away with too much with a familiar dog it will try the same with unknown dogs. If you have a male dog, expect an occasional aggressive incident. If you sense a problem from another male dog, the best policy is avoidance. Play with your dog so he concentrates on you – not the provocateur. There's never any harm in your carrying an ever-ready water pistol for squirting another dog that comes too close. If a fight breaks out, keep your arms and legs out of the melée to avoid heat-of-the-moment bites to you.

'Alice, I think I know what happened to my Viagra...'

Fearful aggression

Fear is the most common reason dogs bite strangers. Fear biting is likely to occur in under-socialized dogs which as pups didn't have the opportunity to meet lots of people. It occurs in dogs who mutter under their breath, 'I am not worthy.' Shy or fearful pups start off life by hiding behind you, running away from what they see as threats or by rolling over to appease when they're frightened. Submissive wetters can turn into fear-biters.

The problem is most acute in breeds prone to emotional stress such as Border collies. In stressful situations, these dogs use aggression to make the 'threat' go away. Watch your dog for signs of fear – body posture, growling, teeth-baring – and eliminate problems before they develop to fear-biting. Allow the fearful dog time to make her own decisions, to be brave enough to come forward on her own to a suitable reward. This means interposing yourself on her behalf to protect her from well-meaning people who try to stroke her or pick her up. Shy dogs need extra attention to reduce their lack of self-confidence.

'Say hello to the nice horsie!'

Predatory aggression

Your dog may look like an angel but she's closer to her roots than you imagine. Dogs chase moving things' that's what they evolved to do. They chase squirrels and rabbits. They chase cats and other dogs. They chase livestock. They chase joggers. They chase bicycles. They chase cars. All dogs chase, but certain breeds – terriers, herders and sight- and scent-hounds in particular – are genetically super-primed for chasing.

For many, the chase itself is the fun. Others enjoy the pounce at the end of the chase, holding down the small dog that has been caught, grabbing the ankle of the jogger. Still others bite after pouncing, killing cats, savaging livestock. This is a primitive and very basic form of aggression and it's potentially there within all dogs.

My retriever is as soft-mouthed and gentle as any dog I've met, but once she's outdoors her instinct to seek out and chase small furries is overwhelming. Macy had delicate hip joints as a pup so I never played toy-retrieval games with her.

I didn't want to overburden her developing joints. I should have.

Channelling a dog's desire to chase into chase-and-retrieve games is the best form of prevention. If your dog chases joggers and bicycles, get friends, armed with water pistols, involved in these activities. When your dog chases, rather than successfully chasing the object away, the jogger or vehicle stops and the dog gets an unexpected shot of water in her face. This is called aversion therapy.

Although there are many different forms of aggression, one type often occurs in synchrony with another. Chase aggression often blends with the desire to protect territory.

Territorial aggression

Your dog is most self-confident on her own territory: your home, garden or car. If she's been well-social-ized to visitors to these areas, she'll not think of strangers as possible threats. Without this early learning, any visitor means potential danger. Barking is the warning and a show of aggression may follow.

Look at these behaviours from your dog's point of view. The mailman comes, makes noise opening the letter box, the dog barks and the mailman leaves. The garbage collectors come, make noise removing the trash, the dog barks and the collectors leave. Guarding and barking works!

'Shut up, Jeeves! It's *me!*'

Prevent (or overcome) this problem by introducing your pup to delivery people, even if it means altering your early morning habits for a while. If you can't do that, talk to your mailman and leave some food treats for him or her to put through the letter box with the mail. If your dog is in the garden when delivery people call, leave a favourite toy or food (in a weatherproof box) at your gate, with instructions for it to be given to your dog when the gate is opened. Your dog will still alert you when someone comes to your house, but she'll not be compulsively protective of your shared territory.

Use the same principle in your car. A car is a small territory: easy to protect. It's your choice how you want you dog to behave there. If you don't want her to be aggressive, nip any potential problems in the bud by avoiding rewards for delinquent behaviour.

Food and toy aggression

'It's mine and you can't touch it!' Don't let your dog get into this habit, which is more common in dogs which as pups had to compete with each other for food. Teach your pup that being touched while eating is OK or that hands near the food bowl will not take food away. When you feed her, kneel down beside her and while she's eating, offer her something even more tasty, such as a meat or a liver treat. After she's used to this, hide the treat in your hand, put your hand in her food bowl and as she noses your hand open it up and give the treat, then let her finish her meal. She'll quickly learn to enjoy your presence rather than feel threatened. Use the same procedure with bones or chew toys she becomes possessive about.

Health-related aggression

If a dog is ill, expect her to be grumpy. If something hurts, her natural response to pain is to bite. These are natural forms of aggression. Be careful when touching or moving an ill or injured dog.

Certain medical conditions are known to be associated with aggression. Some dogs with under-active thyroid glands develop behaviour changes, including aggression. We all know that rabies and aggression go together, but it was only with the advent of magnetic resonance imaging (MRI) scans that veterinarians learned that a variety of older-age behaviour changes including unexpected biting and aggression can be associated with brain tumours.

Learned aggression

There are many different forms of natural aggression but we humans have created one more. Some people like to teach dogs to be aggressive (personally, I think they do so because of that male-overcompensation thing). Leave it to police and other security forces to train dogs to be aggressive.

The best police forces no longer teach predatory aggression to their police dogs; instead they teach 'retrieve'. Whatever the method, after training a dog to attack (or retrieve) someone, the dog will look upon its owner as an excellent pack leader – but what about the rest of the family, neighbours and friends? Once you've let the genie out of the bottle, it can be hard, *really* hard, to get it back in. If you want home protection, train your dog to bark fiercely and invest in an electronic burglar alarm.

How to control delinquency

Neutering means removing the sex-hormone-producing apparatus from the male or female. In males, the testicles are removed. In females, the ovaries are removed. Neutering is still the procedure of choice for preventing unwanted puppies, but it also has effects on the behaviour of males and females.

Male hormone is associated with several dog behaviours. Eliminating (or to be more accurate, dramatically reducing) male hormone is likely to reduce a male dog's need to mark territory frequently with urine, to be aggressive with other male dogs, and to wander over a large territory, preoccupied with sex scents left by other dogs.

Female hormone affects a bitch's personality only during her twice-yearly heat cycles. During that time she urine marks more and wanders more. The hormone of pregnancy (progesterone), which always follows the hormone that stimulates egg release (oestrogen), has a calming effect on behaviour, but it also stimulates a possessive or protective attitude towards her pups or her puppy substitutes such as toys. Neutering eliminates the twice-yearly behaviour changes induced by these hormones. In very rare circumstances, however, in naturally dominant females, the absence of the twice-yearly calming effect of progesterone can exaggerate her natural dominance.

Neutering has no effect on house-guarding, on fear-biting, on predatory aggression or territorial aggression. It has no effect on other aspects of a dog's personality except that dogs pay more attention to people because they're paying less attention to sex-related activity.

If your male dog is aggressive towards other male dogs and you want to find out whether neutering will solve this problem, ask your vet to use hormones to temporarily 'chemically castrate' your dog. This is a safe procedure when used short-term, but these drugs may produce unwanted side effects if used over a prolonged period of time.

Whatever the reason for doing so, neutering just before puberty is an excellent time to carry out this procedure. Early neutering perpetuates the personality as it is. If you like your pup's personality at six months of age, then, subject to your veterinarian agreeing there's no reason why it shouldn't be done, this is when he or she should be neutered.

Each year, millions of people, often children, are bitten by dogs – usually by their own dogs. Some of these bites are fatal. Barbara Woodhouse, the famous English dog trainer wrote a book called *No Bad Dogs*. This is mostly, but not completely, true. There are some bad dogs, bad genes, bad breeding, bad upbringing. Fortunately these are rare.

Most of the dogs euthanized because of aggression could be saved if people understood what was happening before it got so bad that euthanasia became one of the possible outcomes. If your dog shows any signs of aggression, don't wait until the problem gets worse. Muzzle your dog and talk to your vet immediately. He or she will be able to recommend where you can get help to overcome the problem.

'Bad boy, Bogart!'

'Who? Me?'

'When you leave me all day, you
forget that, to a dog, that's *seven* days...'

chapter eight
HOW TO CONTROL OTHER
UNWANTED BEHAVIOURS

Let's be frank. We keep dogs for our benefit, not theirs. We want them to adapt to our standards rather than live to theirs. We get annoyed when our dogs, denied their natural outlets for social interactions with other dogs, denied their need to burn up energy, denied the need to use their brains, howl or bark for companionship, jump on us with excitement or dig to China. These aren't dog problems; they're *our* problems. We provide ourselves with mental, physical and social activity. Do the same with your dog but in dog terms.

Provide mental, physical and social activity

Routine training provides your dog with daily mental stimulation. 'Fetch' is terrific for sedentary owners. Fetch training is quite easy, especially with pups. Begin by throwing a soft toy only a short distance. Let your pup chew on it or do what she wants then get her attention with a 'Come'. As she returns, show her a food reward. As she opens her mouth to get the reward say 'Drop'.

Make sure your dog has mental stimulation when you're absent by providing stimulating toys. Peanut butter or soft cheese in the hollow of a sterilized bone is excellent. So, too, are plastic balls that drop food rewards as they're nosed around the floor.

Let your dog exercise. This is easy. Jogging, bicycling and swimming all are excellent for you. Take your dog along – but be sure to jog or bicycle so that your dog trots rather than runs. Swimming is a great exercise for spaniels and retrievers, although places to swim are limited in urban areas. Only let your dog in a swimming pool that has steps for easy entering and leaving.

Before starting any activity programme, check with your veterinarian about its suitability for your dog, especially if she's small, mature or overweight. And remember, dogs don't sweat the way we do. Never exercise your dog in hot, sunny weather. Always carry water with you, for your dog as well as for you.

Finally, visit the local dog park twice daily to provide your dog with regular social interactions with other dogs. It's amusing, fascinating and socially fulfilling – for both of you.

Expect unwanted behaviours

All dogs develop undesirable habits. Most are minor, but some are so antisocial as to need changing. You can anticipate whether some problems will develop. Read through this list. If your answers are mostly in the left column, the chances of serious problems are much less than if the majority are in the right.

Where did you get your dog?
Breeder/Friend   Ad/Shelter/Pet store

How old was your dog when you acquired him or her?
Under 18 weeks   Over 18 weeks

Has your dog been neutered or will he/she be neutered?
Yes   No

Have you previously owned a dog?
Yes   No

When is your dog fed?
At set times   On demand

Does your dog eat after you?
Yes   No

When does your dog relieve itself?
At set times   No set times

Where does your dog sleep?
Its own bed   On a family bed

How often is your dog groomed?
Frequently   Infrequently

How does your dog react to grooming?
Willingly   Unwillingly

When is your dog exercised
Set times   On demand

How long is the exercise time?
More than one hour/day   Less than one hour/day

Do you have off-leash control?
Yes   No

Where are the dog's toys kept?
In a toy box   On the floor

How often does your dog play with other dogs?
Frequently   Infrequently

How often does your dog meet or play with other people?
Frequently   Infrequently

How long is your dog left at home alone?
Less than four hours   More than four hours

How often does your dog have special playtime with you?
Frequently   Infrequently

Have a plan

Know what you're going to do when problems develop. First, minimize the chance of the problem happening again. For example, if your dog raided the garbage, rather than go through the rigmarole of avoidance training, just move the garbage where it can't be raided. If she's drinking from the toilet, close the lid. Some problems are more likely to occur in one type of dog than another. For example, terriers are inclined to dig. Don't try to overcome this natural behaviour; instead, compromise by redirecting it. Train her to dig only in an approved digging area.

It's difficult to do, but try to avoid unearned rewards. This is easy when the rewards are obvious. If your dog successfully begs at the table, the reward is obvious. Banish the tidbit-giver from the table and the begging stops. Sometimes, however, the reward isn't obvious. If your dog trembles when it sees another dog and you pick her up, you're not reassuring her – you're rewarding her for trembling!

If your dog is chewing a shoe, train your family not to leave shoes about, but leave a chew toy to chew on. If she jumps up to say hello, train her to sit when you come home and reward her for sitting rather than disciplining her for jumping. If she barks when she hears a noise, train her to fetch and carry. It's tough to bark effectively when your mouth is full with a soft toy.

Create circumstances where a dog learns to stop doing something by itself, without your obvious involvement. Use bitter-apple spray, Tabasco sauce or other safe but disagreeable tastes to prevent chewing where you don't want chewing. Use noise the same way. Inexpensive vibration-sensitive alarms for windows, available from most hardware stores, are ideal for putting on beds or sofa if you don't want your dog sleeping on these in your absence. If you're at home and see your dog doing something you don't want her to do, a squirt from your every-ready water pistol or a clunk on the floor from a can filled with a few coins, combined with a verbal 'No!' from you, works wonders. Be creative – and, as always, a little flamboyant.

Follow thoughtful retraining rules

Although bad habits vary, almost all of them can be diminished or corrected following these basic steps:

- Go back to basic obedience. Make sure your dog understands all the basic commands.

- Make sure your dog does something for you, such as sitting or lying down, before she receives any kind of reward, even a verbal 'Hello'.

- Avoid problems. Make sure you can always enforce obedience commands.

- Satisfy your dog's natural needs by creating acceptable outlets for natural behaviour.

- Eliminate the satisfaction your dog gets from her unacceptable behaviour. Sometimes this will involve mild punishment.

- Persevere. Don't expect overnight miracles.

Typically, it takes about three weeks to overcome most common behaviour problems. If you're unsure, or if aggression is involved, get professional help. Don't think professionals will view you as a failure if you ask for advice; asking for help is the surest sign of a commitment to your dog, family and neighbours.

Puppy classes form the basis for good behaviour. Usually available to owners and pups under sixteen weeks old, these weekly classes allow pups to socialize with other pups and with people. Puppy classes provide a secure foundation for future behaviour and for overcoming behaviour problems.

Obedience classes are open to older dogs, but also to pups that have not attended puppy classes. Your veterinary receptionist is well-placed to know who the best trainers are. Alternatively. contact one of the training groups listed under websites at the end of the book.

Advanced training in areas such as agility, games, tracking or canine sports provides an outlet for the natural energy of dogs, especially breeds originally used in these activities. There's nothing better than one-to-one training. If you can afford one, a personal trainer, for you and your dog, is ideal. Ask your veterinarian for advice on who to use. Personal dog trainers are available in virtually all urban areas.

Signs of boredom

•Chewing: doors, wallpaper, rugs, clothing, household linen, car interiors, even themselves. Labradors and Dobermanns are particularly prone to excessively licking their forelegs when they're bored, leading to skin problems needing veterinary attention.

•Digging: in the carpets, in earth or in your bed can be a sign of boredom. Don't, however, mistake boredom digging from digging to bury something or digging to create a cool pit to lie in.

•Howling and barking: when left alone, rather than when she hears a noise. Wolf cubs howl to make contact with mother. Dogs bark out of frustration when separated from you.

•Fence-jumping or rhythmic pacing: in a yard, along a fence, in a garden, or in the house from one window to another. Sometimes pacing is combined with howling, digging, and even urinating.

Ways to prevent boredom – and mayhem

•Before leaving home, make sure your dog has had physical, mental and social activity. Exhausted dogs are much less likely to bark, dig and destroy.

•Feed your dog before you leave. A dog naturally rests when her stomach is full.

•Before you leave, get out a favourite toy, rub it in your hands to leave your scent, and give it to her.

•Always leave quietly. Draw the curtains if necessary and leave a radio or television on to mask distracting noises from outdoors.

•Never leave your dog at home alone all day.

•If you must leave your dog at home alone, get a friend to visit to take your dog for play and exercise. Alternatively, get a dog-walker or drop your dog at a dog day-care centre.

Getting to the root of the problem

At the end of the day, the cure for boredom is to eliminate the cause. If your male dog is barking, digging, destroying or escaping because he is looking for sex, consider neutering him. If your dog is chewing, apply taste-deterrents to objects you don't want chewed.

Use the dog crate constructively if your young dog is simply going through its irritating 'chew-everything' phase which lasts until about eight or nine months of age, but at all times provide exciting chew toys. Dogs need to chew something.

If you have an instinctive digger, redirect her energy away from the flower beds or lawn to an acceptable area. Restrict her to a safe area of the garden and give her a sand pit to dig in.

For fence jumpers, create obstacles. Tin cans strung on a rope about a foot from the fence and three feet off the ground make a nice, noisy and natural deterrent. Chicken wire on the ground at take-off distance from the fence works well, but make sure the gauge of the wire is too small for your dog's foot to slip through.

'Whoa! Just because I'm a dog,
don't think you can cheat!'

The best way to turn off barking is to train your dog to 'Speak' on command. This takes both time and patience.

•Attach your dog's leash to a fence, stand a few feet away and tease her with a toy. When she barks from frustration, give her a food treat. Command 'Speak' the moment she barks, then give the toy as a reward.

'Donald, you're boring the dog again.'

•When she consistently barks to the word 'Speak' for the toy or food, switch to verbal rewards only.

•Once she understands 'Speak', give the command 'Quiet' when she's barking and reward her with the toy or treat as soon as she stops. Be patient. This takes time.

•When she consistently stops barking when you say 'Quiet', move a short distance away and repeat the exercise, returning to her initially with a food or toy reward. Eventually switch to verbal rewards at a distance when she responds to your 'Quiet' command.

•Finally, set up mock departures, giving the 'quiet' command before you leave. Stand outside the door. If she barks, make a noise; for example, drop an aluminium pan to startle her into not barking. Return and praise her for being quiet.

Excitement can be controlled

Dogs show they're excited in different ways: by barking, pulling on the leash, jumping and wanting to lick your face, nipping with excitement, even chasing their own tails. Active exercise and good basic obedience training are at the root of preventing over-excited behaviour. Plan ahead. If your dog jumps on visitors to greet them, make sure she's on a leash, or in another room when visitors come into your home. If she pulls on the leash, don't turn this into a game of tug-of-war. Instead:

- Go back to basics until you're sure your dog follows basic obedience signals.

- Proceed to basic walking to heel retraining but now, with her on her leash at your left, slide your left hand down the leash to near her collar and if she pulls, pull back firmly and command her to 'Sit'.

- Start again, giving the 'Heel' command. If she pulls, give another yank and command to 'Sit'.

•Repeat this exercise until she walks quietly without pulling. Reward her with a food treat.

•Graduate to more distracting environments and circumstances.

If your dog jumps on you, it's better to give a positive command ('Sit') than a negative one ('Off'). If your dog thinks she's a canine missile, aiming her tongue at your mouth each time you come home, just ignore the flamboyant greeting. Avoid eye contact and go about your business until all four of her feet are back on the ground. Don't raise your voice, wave your aims or in any other way increase her excitement. Only then give the command 'Sit' and reward her with a quiet 'Hello'. Praise calm obedience.

Young dogs, terriers in particular, tend to tug on clothes, or your body parts, when excited. Overcome this unpleasant habit by training your dog to carry a toy in her mouth. If she's preoccupied with one job, then it's difficult to carry out another. Try to integrate toy-carrying with basic 'sit-stay' obedience. Toy-carrying is also a wonderful way to muffle barking. To control barking itself, follow the same procedure for controlling boredom barking.

Dogs behave the way they do because they're members of the intelligent, sociable and adaptable canine family of mammals. They've got the ability to behave in ways we want them to because of their malleable, impressionable and plastic minds. Remember, there are limits to what they can do. Don't have unwarranted expectations about what your dog is capable of.

If your ambitions for your dog are realistic, however, there's not a better or more satisfying companion anywhere in the animal world.

Useful contacts

Veterinary associations

American Animal Hospital Association
www.healthypet.com

American Veterinary Medical Association
www.avma.org

British Small Animal Veterinary Association
www.bsava.com

British Veterinary Association
www.bva.co.uk

Canadian Veterinary Medical Association
www.cvma-acmv.org

Federation of European Companion Animal
Veterinary Associations
www.fecava.org

Dog welfare

The Blue Cross (UK)
www.bluecross.org.uk

BVA Animal Welfare Association (UK)
www.bva-awf.org

The Humane Society of the United States
www.hsus.org

Dogs Trust (UK)
www.dogstrust.co.uk

Royal Society for the Prevention of Cruelty to Animals (UK)
www.rspca.org.uk

Dog training and activity associations

USA AND CANADA
Association of Pet Dog Trainers
www.apdt.com

National Association of Dog Obedience Instructors
www.nadoi.org

North American Dog Agility Council
www.nadac.com

North American Flyball Association
www.flyball.org

US Dog Agility Association
www.usdaa.com

UK AND REPUBLIC OF IRELAND
Association of Pet Behaviour Councellors
www.apbc.org

Association of Pet Dog Trainers
www.apdt.co.uk

The Kennel Club (UK)
www.the-kennel-club.org.uk

Index